BORED OF DIRECTORS

A PRACTICAL HANDBOOK FOR HIGH-PERFORMING BOARDS

JISHORE ABIC

ISBN
Hardcase 979-8-89724-798-1
Paperback 979-8-89673-484-0

DEDICATED TO

This book is dedicated to:

- CXOs and Senior Leaders: Who navigate the ever-evolving challenges of leadership and seek clarity and direction in the boardroom.
- Entrepreneurs: Who dare to dream, build, and scale, yet often grapple with the complexities of governance and strategy.
- Family Business Owners: Who balance tradition and innovation while striving for sustainable success and professionalised governance.
- Chartered Accountants and Finance Professionals: Both young and seasoned, who aim to transition from technical experts to strategic boardroom influencers.
- Experienced Directors and Aspiring Board Members: Who seek to sharpen their perspectives, question the status quo, and create a lasting impact.
- To all those who find themselves at a crossroads in their leadership journey—this book is for you, to inspire, guide, and reignite the passion for purposeful governance and impactful decision-making.

Table of Contents

About the Author

Jishore Abic's remarkable journey from a small village in Kerala to becoming one of the most respected financial leaders in the Middle East is a powerful testament to his resilience, determination, and visionary leadership. With over 25 years of experience, Jishore has firmly established himself as one of the most sought-after CFOs and Board Advisers in the region, recognised for his strategic foresight and exceptional ability to deliver impactful results. In 2024, Jishore was recognised as one of the Global Power Leaders in Finance, a prestigious accolade that celebrates his significant contributions to the field of financial leadership and corporate governance.

Having lived in Dubai, UAE, for the past 21 years, Jishore's career has been defined by significant achievements, particularly in the areas of mergers, acquisitions, business restructuring, and corporate governance. As the Chief Financial Officer (CFO), he has been instrumental in driving organisational transformation, steering the company towards sustainable growth and operational excellence.

Driven by the philosophy that "success is the sum of small efforts, repeated day in and day out", Jishore has continually pursued excellence and professional growth throughout his career. His innovative approach to financial leadership has set new benchmarks, particularly within the healthcare sector in the Middle East.

Jishore is a Fellow Chartered Accountant (FCA) from the Institute of Chartered Accountants of India and holds a diploma in IFRS from the Association of Chartered Certified Accountants (UK). A mathematics prodigy, he earned 100% marks and a Gold Medal from Mahatma Gandhi University, India.

Jishore is supported by his wife, Rosemary, and their two children—Jonathan and Agnella. His family has been a constant source of inspiration and strength throughout his personal and professional journey.

As the author of BORED of DIRECTORS, Jishore shares the wealth of knowledge and insights gained throughout his distinguished career. This marks his first book, where he delves into the critical role of directors, corporate governance, and the best practices that drive organisational success. Drawing from years of hands-on experience, Jishore offers invaluable guidance to leaders and organisations, helping them navigate the complexities of effective governance and leadership in today's dynamic business environment.

CA. JISHORE M ABIC
FCA | FFA | FIPA | CPFA | DipIFRS | UAECA | BSc Maths
Email: jish.abic@gmail.com
Mob +971 55 166 0188

Preface

In BORED of DIRECTORS, I aim to demystify the enigma of boardrooms and the often complex dynamics of corporate governance. This book is not just another manual; it's a ready reckoner for anyone navigating the multifaceted corridors of leadership—be it CXOs, entrepreneurs, family business owners, young and seasoned chartered accountants, or those who feel stuck after years in the C-suite. Whether you're an aspiring board member, a family business leader striving for structured governance, or an experienced director questioning your next move, this book is for you.

The title, BORED of DIRECTORS, reflects the disillusionment that many leaders experience after spending years in leadership roles. A sense of stagnation often creeps in—questions arise, ambitions waver, and purpose feels elusive. I've been there, and I know what it takes to reignite the spark.

Through this book, I take you on a transformative journey into the heart of boardroom dynamics, sharing real-life stories, hard-earned lessons, and actionable strategies. Drawing from over two decades of experience across diverse industries, I explore the untold truths of directorship and corporate governance. From navigating power dynamics to driving strategic impact, this guide serves as your compass to excel in boardroom leadership.

Why This Book, Why Now?

In a world where businesses are transforming at breakneck speed, the role of directors is more critical than ever. The modern boardroom is no longer a passive environment; it demands agility, accountability, and strategic foresight. Yet, most leaders enter the boardroom unprepared for its challenges. I wrote this book to bridge that gap—to empower leaders with insights that transform potential into impact.

Each chapter is designed as a practical resource enriched with templates, frameworks, and best practices that you can immediately implement. This is not a book to skim; it's a guide to revisit, annotate, and apply. Whether you're preparing for your first board meeting or striving to steer an organisation through turbulent waters, you'll find answers here.

What to Expect?

1. Real-World Insights: From navigating crises to driving innovation, I share key experiences that highlight pivotal moments and real-world examples. Although space limits the inclusion of detailed case studies, the insights presented capture the core lessons and practical strategies derived from these transformative events.
2. Comprehensive Guides: Practical tools such as board evaluation templates, director onboarding frameworks, and corporate governance checklists are laid out with clarity and purpose.
3. Inspiring Lessons: I interweave lessons from mentors, peers, and personal trials, creating a narrative that is as engaging as it is informative.
4. For Every Leader: Whether you are climbing the corporate ladder or seeking to leave a lasting legacy, this book caters to leaders at every stage of their journey.

My Promise to You

This book is not just about navigating the boardroom; it's about rekindling purpose. It's about breaking free from the monotony that often seeps into leadership roles and rediscovering the passion that got you here in the first place. As you turn these pages, I promise you a blend of knowledge, wisdom, and inspiration that will empower you to lead with courage, integrity, and impact.

Final Thoughts

As a boy who once dreamt beyond the limits of his surroundings, and as a professional who faced both triumphs and trials, my journey has been nothing short of extraordinary. BORED of DIRECTORS is a testament to that journey—a guide for all those who seek to rise above mediocrity and make a meaningful difference.

So, welcome to this transformative journey. Let's turn boredom into brilliance and together redefine what it means to lead.

– **Jishore Abic**
Author, thought leader and
advocate for purposeful leadership

Acknowledgements

Writing BORED of DIRECTORS has been a transformative journey, and it would not have been possible without the unwavering support, guidance, and inspiration from the remarkable individuals who have touched my life.

First and foremost, I am deeply grateful to my parents, Abraham and Mariamma, who instilled in me the values of hard work, resilience, and humility. Their sacrifices and encouragement have been the foundation of everything I have achieved.

To my wife, Rosemary, and my children, Jonathan and Agnella, your love, patience, and unwavering belief in me have been my greatest source of strength. You have been my anchor and my inspiration throughout this journey.

I owe a debt of gratitude to my mentors, whose wisdom and guidance have shaped my career and character. Your teachings have been invaluable, and your belief in my potential has always motivated me to strive for excellence.

To my teachers, who sparked my love for learning and nurtured my passion for numbers, and to my colleagues at work who have collaborated with me through challenges and successes—thank you for your insights, support, and camaraderie.

A special thanks to my finance, accounts, and audit teams, whose dedication, professionalism, and commitment have been instrumental in achieving the goals we set together. You have been a true embodiment of teamwork and perseverance.

To my friends and well-wishers, who have stood by me through every milestone, your encouragement and positivity have always reminded me of the importance of meaningful relationships.

Lastly, but most importantly, I extend my heartfelt thanks to all my future board members—those aspiring, those already in the boardroom, and those who will redefine what effective leadership looks like. This book is my gift to you, a guide to navigating the complexities of governance with confidence and clarity.

To all of you, thank you for being part of my journey. This book is a reflection of your influence and a testament to the collective wisdom that surrounds me. I hope BORED of DIRECTORS serves as a source of inspiration and empowerment, just as you have been for me.

With deepest gratitude,
Jishore Abic

"You don't have to be great to start, but you have to start to be great."

– Zig Ziglar

Introduction: Guiding Through the Storm: How Boards Shape Business Futures

Over coffee at a cosy café in City Walk, a popular spot in Dubai, a group of young entrepreneur friends shared their excitement about a groundbreaking product they had just launched. Their enthusiasm was infectious, but so was the underlying anxiety. "We're juggling hiring, marketing, scaling, and finances," one of them confessed, absentmindedly stirring their coffee.

When I suggested forming a board of directors, they looked puzzled. "Why would we need a board? Isn't that just for big corporations?"

I leant forward, smiling. "Let me share something with you," I began. "Throughout my career, I've encountered countless stories—some I've been part of, others I've studied closely—where a board of directors was the deciding factor between success and failure. A strong board isn't a luxury; it's a cornerstone for growth, sustainability, and long-term vision. Whether you're a startup or a global enterprise, the right board can shape your future in extraordinary ways."

That moment crystallised the motivation behind this book. It isn't just a guide – it's a journey through real-life experiences, case studies, and actionable insights. As someone who has spent decades in finance, corporate governance, and strategic advisory, I've seen first-hand how boards drive innovation, challenge assumptions, and safeguard companies through turbulent times. This book is my way of sharing those lessons, presenting practical advice, and equipping today's leaders with the tools to build boards that transform their organisations.

Welcome to BORED of DIRECTORS, a comprehensive guide that bridges theory and practice, filled with stories, examples, and strategies to empower directors, executives, and aspiring entrepreneurs. Let's explore a few introductory stories, keeping in mind that the companies and characters are purely fictional. These narratives are crafted to provide insights into the significance of a board and its pivotal role in steering organisational success.

Take the case of Bluewave Innovations. Back in 2007, this promising mid-sized tech startup was riding high on the success of its flagship software. Ethan, the founder, was a brilliant tech visionary whose ability to design cutting-edge algorithms and sleek user interfaces earned widespread admiration. But while Ethan excelled at product development, his grasp of business strategy left much to be desired.

As the company expanded, cracks began to show. A botched product launch drained their cash reserves, and a poorly executed marketing campaign alienated loyal customers. On the verge of collapse, Ethan realised he couldn't save Bluewave on his own. In a bold move, he formed a board of directors, bringing together experienced entrepreneurs, a retired CFO, and an industry consultant.

At their first meeting, the board quickly identified a root issue: Ethan's micromanagement had stifled his team and slowed decision-making. The board implemented governance practices, streamlined operations, and secured critical investment. Within a year, Bluewave stabilised and then thrived, ultimately becoming a leader in its niche market.

Now contrast that with Stonehill Foods, a once-thriving family-owned business in the food industry. Proud of their legacy, the founding family refused to consider external oversight. They believed they could handle all decisions themselves, relying on tradition and intuition. But a series of missteps—poor market positioning and an inability to adapt to evolving consumer trends—led to declining revenues and mounting debt. A public scandal over mismanagement was the final blow. Without a board to challenge their assumptions or provide guidance, Stonehill

Foods became a cautionary tale of a beloved brand that could have been saved.

This brings us to NovaTech Systems, another tech company that faced a turning point. Founded by Lucas in 2010, NovaTech started strong but soon faltered. Lucas, a gifted coder, struggled with scaling operations and developing a broader business strategy. As revenues plateaued and competitors gained ground, Lucas realised he needed help. He assembled a formal board, including Samantha, a retired CFO renowned for turning around struggling businesses.

At the first meeting, Samantha identified a critical flaw: Lucas made decisions based on instinct, not data. She proposed robust financial reporting systems and restructuring the management team to include seasoned professionals. Over two years, NovaTech not only recovered but also flourished, becoming a market leader and eventually going public. It was a testament to the transformative power of a well-assembled board.

Unfortunately, not every company embraces this wisdom. GreenFields Organics, a family-run agricultural business, refused to adapt. When the market shifted towards sustainable practices, the founders dismissed the idea of forming a board, relying instead on their traditional ways. Without anyone to challenge their outdated assumptions or guide a strategic pivot, the company floundered and filed for bankruptcy within five years.

Finally, there's Stratford Textiles, a family-owned company that was celebrated as an industry leader until the market evolved and left them behind. By 2012, the founder—a master craftsman but not a strategist—was overwhelmed by the complexities of digital transformation, supply chain optimisation, and global expansion. When a trusted adviser suggested forming a board of directors, the founder resisted, scoffing, *"Why pay outsiders to tell me how to run my business?"*

But desperation eventually pushed him to recruit a board comprising an industry veteran, a tech-savvy entrepreneur, and a financial strategist.

Within six months, the company had a clear modernisation roadmap. Two years later, Stratford Textiles not only survived but reclaimed its position as a market leader, all thanks to the accountability and expertise of its board.

In many family businesses, key roles are often entrusted to relatives who have a deep connection to the enterprise's success. However, this close association can sometimes make it challenging for them to question decisions or present alternative perspectives. This dynamic, while rooted in trust and loyalty, can unintentionally create an environment where oversight is limited, and critical decisions may go unchallenged—even when they deviate from the company's best interests.

Introducing independent and non-executive directors can be a pivotal step in addressing this governance gap. These directors bring an objective and impartial perspective, unclouded by familial ties or internal dependencies. Their role is not to override the authority of the business owner but to enhance decision-making by fostering open dialogue, strategic deliberation, and accountability. With their external expertise and unbiased insights, independent and non-executive directors contribute to aligning decisions with the long-term objectives of the business.

It is natural for business owners, particularly those with a strong vision and confidence in their leadership, to be cautious about inviting external perspectives into the decision-making process. Yet, having worked with numerous family businesses, I have observed that openness often results in significant benefits. The inclusion of independent voices leads to better oversight, innovative thinking, and a more resilient governance structure—ultimately reinforcing the business's legacy and setting the stage for sustained growth. When business owners embrace this collaborative approach, they safeguard their company's future and create a lasting foundation for the generations to come.

Whether of success or failure, these stories reveal a universal truth: a board of directors is essential for any business aiming to navigate challenges, seize opportunities, and achieve sustained growth. A board offers the *"why"*—ensuring accountability and long-term success. It defines the *"what"*—evolving into a strategic asset. It underscores the *"when"*—demonstrating its importance at every stage of growth, from startups to family businesses to large enterprises. It embodies the *"how"* of assembling a diverse, skilled team that can guide organisations through crises, drive innovation, and unlock their full potential.

What Is a Board of Directors?

Picture this: a company is like a ship navigating uncharted waters. The CEO is at the helm, steering the wheel, but the board of directors act as the crew in the crow's nest, spotting distant dangers and opportunities.

At its core, a board of directors is a group of individuals responsible for overseeing a company's governance, strategy, and long-term success. While the CEO and management handle day-to-day operations, the board ensures the organisation stays true to its mission and adapts to an ever-changing environment.

The concept of a board dates back centuries. In the 17th century, as trade expanded globally, corporations like the East India Company were formed. Shareholders who couldn't directly oversee operations entrusted boards to represent their interests. Over time, the role of boards evolved beyond shareholder protection to include safeguarding the interests of employees, customers, and society at large.

In today's world, boards are no longer passive overseers. They're active partners, balancing governance with strategic insight, ensuring that companies not only survive but thrive in a competitive landscape.

Why Do Companies Need a Board of Directors?

Let's return to our ship metaphor. Without a competent crew, even the most skilled captain risks running aground. Similarly, companies without effective boards often lack the guidance and oversight needed to navigate challenges.

Here are three key reasons why boards are indispensable:

1. **Governance and Accountability:** Boards ensure that companies operate ethically, legally, and transparently. They establish checks and balances, preventing mismanagement and fostering trust among stakeholders.
2. **Strategic Oversight:** Boards bring a wealth of experience and diverse perspectives to the table. They help management think long-term, identify growth opportunities, and adapt to market changes.
3. **Risk Mitigation:** From financial risks to reputational threats, boards play a critical role in identifying and mitigating potential pitfalls. Their oversight helps companies stay resilient in uncertain times.

Take the example of Ford Motor Company. In the early 2000s, the company struggled with declining sales and an outdated product lineup. Alan Mulally, the then-CEO, credits Ford's turnaround to a supportive and strategic board that backed his decision to streamline operations and focus on core models.

Contrast this with the infamous Enron scandal, where a lack of effective board oversight allowed fraudulent practices to go unchecked, leading to one of the largest corporate bankruptcies in history.

When Should a Company Plan for a Board of Directors?

The question of *when* to establish a board is as crucial as deciding *who* should sit on it. The answer depends on the company's stage of growth and specific needs:

- **Startups:** Early-stage companies often rely on informal advisers, but as they scale, formalising a board becomes essential. A board lends credibility, attracts investors, and ensures that the founder's vision aligns with market realities.

- **Family Businesses:** Family-run enterprises often face unique challenges, such as succession planning and balancing personal dynamics with professional decisions. A board provides objectivity, helping to professionalise operations and plan for the future.
- **Small and Medium Enterprises (SMEs):** For SMEs, boards bring expertise and networks that the management team may lack. They're instrumental in helping businesses expand regionally or internationally.
- **Large Corporations:** In established companies, boards play a critical role in governance, risk management, and ensuring that the organisation remains agile in a competitive market.

Consider the case of Eco Light, a sustainable energy startup. When its founder, Maria, secured Series A funding, the investors insisted on forming a board. Initially sceptical, Maria soon realised the value of having seasoned professionals guide her through regulatory hurdles and market entry strategies. Today, Eco Light is a leading player in the renewable energy sector.

The Critical Moments That Define a Board

Boards are often judged by how they respond during pivotal moments. Let's explore three scenarios that illustrate their impact:

1. **Crisis Management:** In 2017, a cybersecurity breach rocked a major retail chain. The board stepped in immediately, assembling a crisis management team and hiring experts to rebuild the company's security systems. Their swift action not only minimised damage but also restored customer trust.
2. **Strategic Pivot:** A traditional publishing house faced declining revenues as digital media disrupted the industry. The board's deep understanding of market trends enabled them to guide

the company toward a subscription-based model, securing its survival.

3. **Ethical Oversight:** A beverage company was accused of unethical sourcing practices. The board launched an independent investigation and implemented strict supply chain policies, salvaging the brand's reputation.

These examples highlight why boards matter. They provide the expertise, objectivity, and foresight that can make or break a company.

A Call to Action: Boards as Strategic Assets

Despite their importance, boards are often misunderstood. Some view them as ceremonial bodies, convening only to approve decisions already made. Others see them as obstacles, hindering management's freedom to act.

It's time to change that narrative.

A well-structured board isn't a formality – it's a strategic asset. It's a team of mentors, challengers, and collaborators who can elevate a company to new heights.

As you delve into this book, you'll discover not only the *what* and *why* of boards but also the *how*—how to build them, how to lead them, and how to harness their full potential.

Whether you're an entrepreneur contemplating your first board, a seasoned director seeking fresh perspectives, or a business leader navigating complex challenges, this book is your guide.

Let's reimagine boards as catalysts for growth, innovation, and resilience. Let's move from *bored* to *brilliant*. The journey starts now.

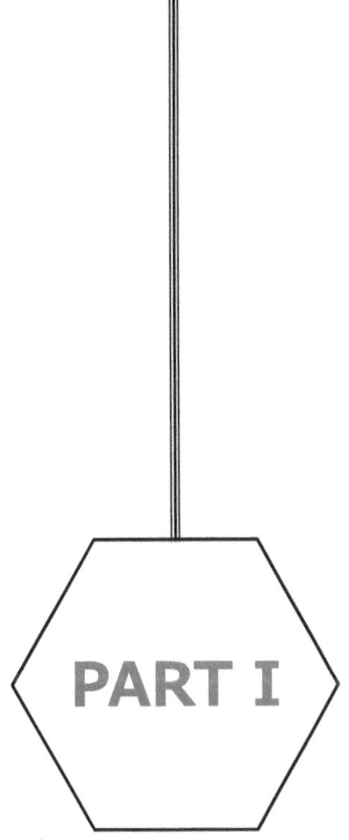

Understanding the Role of Directors

Chapter 1

The Evolution of the Board of Directors

Why Understanding the Evolution of Boards Matters

The role of the board of directors is central to the governance and success of modern organisations. However, this role did not always exist in its current form. By examining the historical evolution of boards, directors can gain valuable insights into their responsibilities, the challenges they face, and the best practices they should adopt. This chapter explores how boards have evolved from informal advisory groups to formalised governance bodies, providing the foundation for modern corporate governance.

Early Governance Models: Foundations of the Board

In the pre-industrial era, governance often revolved around sole proprietorships and partnerships. Decision-making was concentrated in the hands of business owners, with minimal oversight or accountability to external parties.

1. **The Dutch East India Company (1602): The First Corporate Board**

    The establishment of the Dutch East India Company marked a pivotal moment in governance. As the first publicly traded company, it introduced the concept of external shareholders and necessitated a governing body to oversee operations. This led to the creation of one of the earliest boards of directors, tasked with protecting shareholder interests while ensuring operational efficiency.

Key takeaway: The need for accountability to external stakeholders gave rise to the concept of governance through boards.

2. **Industrial Revolution (18th-19th Century): Formalising Governance Structures**

    The rapid expansion of businesses during the Industrial Revolution highlighted the limitations of owner-driven governance. Companies required more structured oversight, leading to the formal establishment of boards composed of directors who could provide strategic guidance and operational oversight.

Real-world example: British railway companies were among the first to adopt formal boards to manage large-scale infrastructure projects and public investments.

Modern Corporate Structures: The Evolution of Board Roles

The 20th century saw the board's role evolve significantly, influenced by changes in business complexity, regulatory environments, and societal expectations.

1. **Post-World War II: Accountability and Shareholder Value**

    - Corporations grew larger, with boards focusing on delivering value to shareholders.
    - Regulatory developments, such as the creation of the U.S. Securities and Exchange Commission (SEC) in 1934, emphasised transparency and accountability.

2. **Late 20ᵗʰ Century: Stakeholder Governance**

    - Growing awareness of environmental, social, and governance (ESG) issues shifted board focus beyond just shareholder interests to include stakeholders like employees, customers, and communities.
    - Case study: **Johnson & Johnson's Credo:** During the 1982 Tylenol crisis, Johnson & Johnson's board demonstrated strong governance by prioritising public safety over short-term profits, aligning with its corporate credo.

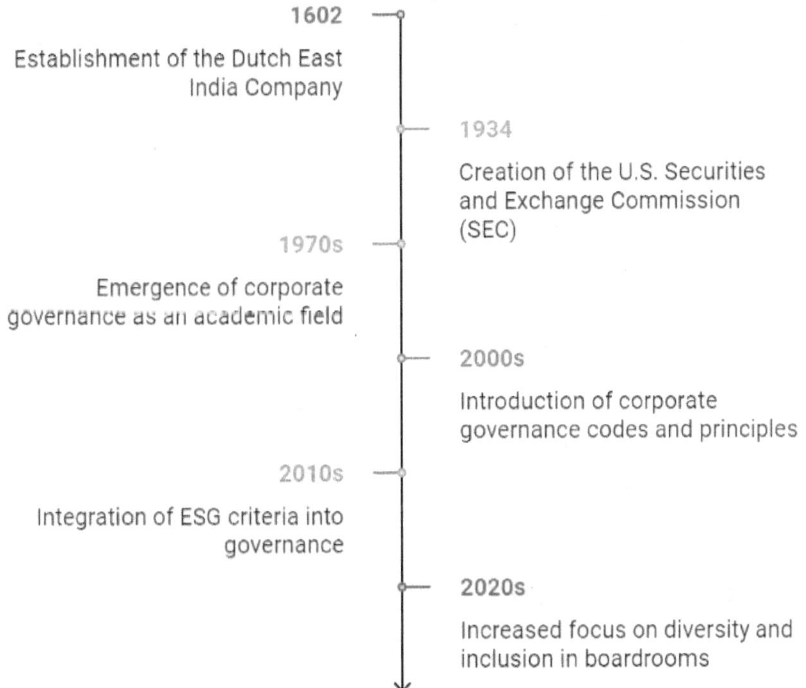

Case Study: General Electric's Board Transformation

The Challenge:

In the late 20th century, General Electric (GE) faced challenges as its board struggled to adapt to global competition and regulatory changes.

The Transformation:

Under the leadership of Jack Welch, GE's board underwent a transformation:

- Independent directors were appointed to provide unbiased oversight.
- Committees were established to focus on critical areas like audit and executive compensation.
- Board meetings became more structured, with clear agendas and decision-making frameworks.

The Outcome:

GE became a model for governance, demonstrating how a proactive board could drive innovation and resilience.

Practical Tips for Modern Directors

Understanding the evolution of boards provides actionable insights for current and aspiring directors:

1. **Embrace Continuous Education**

   - Directors should stay updated on governance trends, regulatory changes, and industry practices.
   - Example: Attending workshops or enrolling in corporate governance certifications.

2. **Adopt a Stakeholder-Centric Approach**

   - Consider the interests of all stakeholders, not just shareholders.

- Example: Integrating ESG metrics into board evaluations and decision-making processes.

3. **Foster Independence**

   - Ensure the board includes independent directors to enhance objectivity.
   - Best practice: Regularly review the independence of board members and mitigate conflicts of interest.

4. **Leverage Technology**

   - Use digital tools for better decision-making, such as data analytics platforms and board management software.
   - Example: Virtual board meetings and secure online portals for document sharing.

Interactive Element: Quiz and Discussion

Quiz: How Well Do You Know Board Evolution?

1. Which company is credited with creating the first board of directors?

   a) British East India Company
   b) Dutch East India Company
   c) General Electric
   d) Johnson & Johnson

2. What was the primary focus of boards during the Industrial Revolution?

   a) Maximising shareholder value
   b) Managing large-scale operations
   c) Addressing ESG issues
   d) Establishing employee benefits

Discussion Question:

Imagine you are part of a 21st-century board tasked with navigating an ESG crisis. How would you balance stakeholder expectations while ensuring the company's financial sustainability?

Key Takeaways

1. The concept of a board of directors emerged from the need for accountability and strategic oversight in complex organisations.
2. Historical shifts, such as the Industrial Revolution and the rise of regulatory bodies, shaped the modern board's structure and responsibilities.
3. Modern boards must adopt a holistic approach, balancing shareholder interests with those of stakeholders.
4. Directors can benefit from understanding the historical evolution of boards to navigate current challenges effectively.

By tracing the evolution of boards, this chapter provides directors with the context and tools they need to lead with insight and responsibility.

Chapter 2

The Role of Directors Today

Why Directors' Roles Are More Critical Than Ever

The responsibilities of directors have expanded and evolved in response to the complexities of modern businesses and global markets. Today's directors are not only strategists but also custodians of governance, risk managers, and champions of stakeholder interests. Their decisions significantly influence an organisation's financial health, reputation, and long-term success. Understanding the multifaceted role of directors is essential for fostering effective governance and driving sustainable growth.

Core Responsibilities of Directors

1. **Strategic Responsibilities**

   Directors play a critical role in shaping the strategic direction of an organisation. They collaborate with management to set long-term goals, assess market trends, and ensure the company remains competitive.

   - **Example:** A board devising a five-year growth strategy for a tech startup must evaluate risks such as rapid technological obsolescence and funding challenges.

2. **Oversight Responsibilities**

   Directors oversee management's execution of the strategy, ensuring accountability, compliance, and operational efficiency. This involves monitoring key performance indicators (KPIs), evaluating executive leadership, and addressing deviations from the strategic plan.

- ○ **Example:** A board overseeing a manufacturing company may track metrics like production efficiency, supply chain sustainability, and ESG compliance.

3. **Risk Management Responsibilities**

Identifying, assessing, and mitigating risks is a fundamental duty of directors. Boards are tasked with ensuring the organisation has a robust risk management framework to address financial, operational, reputational, and cybersecurity risks.

- ○ **Example:** In the face of a data breach, a director must collaborate with management to implement immediate damage control and enhance cybersecurity protocols.

4. **Fiduciary Responsibilities**

Directors must act in the best interests of the company and its stakeholders. This includes duties of care, loyalty, and obedience to the organisation's mission and regulatory requirements.

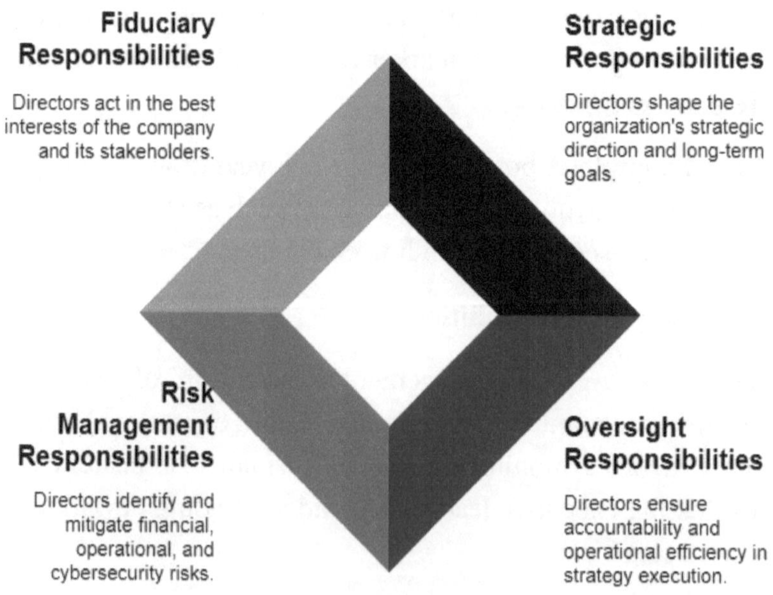

Duties Under Law and Corporate Frameworks

1. **Legal Duties of Directors**

    Across jurisdictions, directors have defined legal obligations. For example:

    a) **Duty of Care:** Directors must make informed decisions based on adequate analysis.
    b) **Duty of Loyalty:** Directors must prioritise the company's interests over personal gain.
    c) **Duty of Obedience:** Directors must ensure the organisation complies with laws and regulations.

    Real-world example: The Enron scandal highlighted how breaches of fiduciary duties can lead to catastrophic outcomes for organisations and stakeholders.

Table: Legal Duties Across Jurisdictions

Legal Duty	U.S.	UK	UAE
Fiduciary Duty	Act in the best interests of the company	Same as U.S.	Same as U.S.
Duty of Care	Act with the care an ordinary prudent person would	Similar to U.S., with additional statutory duties	Enforced through UAE Companies Law
Duty of Loyalty	Avoid conflicts of interest	Same as U.S., with additional statutory duties	Same as U.S., regulated by Companies Law
Duty to Act Lawfully	Comply with all applicable laws and regulations	Extensive compliance requirements	Similar to U.S. and UK, with local compliance
Duty of Confidentiality	Protect sensitive company information	Similar to U.S.	Similar to U.S. and UK

2. **Corporate Governance Frameworks**

Governance frameworks provide the structure within which directors fulfil their roles. These include board charters, codes of conduct, and performance evaluation mechanisms.

Example: The Organisation for Economic Co-operation and Development (OECD) Principles of Corporate Governance emphasise transparency, accountability, and shareholder rights as pillars for effective board practices.

Case Study: Navigating a Complex Decision

Scenario:

A mid-sized retail company faced declining revenues due to changing consumer preferences and the rise of e-commerce. The board had to decide whether to pivot to an online-first strategy or invest in reinvigorating physical stores.

Board's Role:

1. **Strategic Analysis:** The board evaluated market trends, competitive benchmarks, and customer feedback.
2. **Risk Assessment:** Directors identified risks such as increased capital requirements for digital transformation and the potential alienation of loyal brick-and-mortar customers.
3. **Decision-Making:** After multiple discussions, the board approved a hybrid strategy, allocating resources to both enhance e-commerce capabilities and revitalise key stores.
4. **Outcome:** The dual approach stabilised revenues and restored shareholder confidence, showcasing the board's ability to navigate a complex, high-stakes decision.

Practical Tips for Directors

1. **Develop a Strategic Mindset**

    - Regularly review industry trends and anticipate potential disruptions.
    - Foster a collaborative relationship with management to align strategic priorities.

2. **Enhance Oversight Practices**

    - Establish clear performance benchmarks and review them periodically.
    - Encourage management to present alternative viewpoints and scenarios.

3. **Prioritise Ethical Leadership**

    - Uphold transparency and integrity in all board dealings.
    - Lead by example in adhering to the organisation's code of conduct.

4. **Focus on Continuous Learning**

    - Attend governance workshops, seminars, and training sessions.
    - Engage with peer networks to exchange best practices and lessons learned.

Interactive Element: Checklist and Discussion Questions

Checklist for Directors:

1. Have I reviewed all relevant materials and data before making decisions?
2. Am I acting in the best interests of the organisation and its stakeholders?

3. Does the company have a clear risk management framework in place?

4. Have I evaluated management's performance against agreed KPIs?

Discussion Question:

As a director, how would you balance short-term shareholder expectations with long-term sustainability goals?

Key Takeaways

1. Modern directors must balance strategic, oversight, and fiduciary responsibilities to drive organisational success.
2. Legal duties like the duty of care, loyalty, and obedience guide directors in fulfilling their roles ethically and effectively.
3. Governance frameworks and continuous education are vital for equipping directors to face evolving challenges.
4. Practical tools, such as checklists and risk management frameworks, enhance board decision-making.

By understanding and embracing these roles, directors can contribute significantly to the organisation's strategic vision, resilience, and governance excellence.

Chapter 3

Types of Directors

The Relevance of Director Types in Corporate Governance

The board of directors is the cornerstone of corporate governance, serving as a critical body that shapes the direction and integrity of an organisation. However, not all directors play the same role. Understanding the different types of directors—executive, non-executive, and independent—is crucial for fostering a balanced, effective, and accountable board. Each type brings unique perspectives, skills, and responsibilities, which collectively contribute to sound decision-making and governance.

In recent years, high-profile corporate failures have underscored the importance of clearly defined director roles. For example, the collapse of Enron and Lehman Brothers revealed governance gaps, partly due to ineffective board structures. By understanding these roles, directors can navigate potential conflicts of interest, ensure a diversity of thought, and uphold fiduciary responsibilities.

Example: A Tale of Success and Failure in Director Dynamics

The downfall of Theranos serves as a cautionary tale about the dangers of ineffective board governance. Despite having a high-profile board composed of distinguished individuals, many of its directors lacked the relevant expertise in biotechnology and healthcare to critically evaluate the company's claims and strategies. The board often failed to exercise independent judgement, and its oversight role was diminished by an over-reliance on the company's founder, Elizabeth Holmes. This lack of accountability and expertise contributed to one of the most high-profile corporate collapses in recent history.

In contrast, the turnaround of Netflix during the 2010s under Reed Hastings exemplifies the power of an engaged and well-composed board. Facing intense competition and the need to transition from a DVD rental service to a streaming platform, Netflix's board included a mix of executives and independent directors with diverse expertise in technology, media, and finance. These directors played a critical role in challenging assumptions, providing strategic insights, and supporting bold decisions such as investing in original content.

This governance structure fostered a culture of accountability and innovation, helping Netflix become a global leader in the entertainment industry.

These contrasting stories highlight how the composition and dynamics of a board can shape organisational outcomes. While weak governance can lead to catastrophic failures, a balanced, skilled, and engaged board can drive transformative success.

Types of Directors

1. **Executive Directors**

    Executive directors are members of the board who are also part of the company's management team. They are actively involved in day-to-day operations and bring in-depth knowledge of the business to the boardroom.

    o   **Roles and Responsibilities**

    -   Setting and executing the company's strategic goals.
    -   Acting as a bridge between the board and management.
    -   Ensuring operational decisions align with the board's vision.

    o   **Importance**

    Executive directors provide the board with first-hand insights into operational challenges and opportunities, enabling informed decision-making.

- o **Example:**

  Satya Nadella, CEO and executive director of Microsoft, revitalised the company by championing a culture of innovation and aligning board objectives with operational strategies.

2. **Non-Executive Directors (NEDs)**

Non-executive directors are not part of the company's management. They contribute an independent perspective and focus on oversight rather than operations.

- o **Roles and Responsibilities**

  - Challenging and supporting executive management.
  - Monitoring the organisation's performance against strategic goals.
  - Representing stakeholder interests.

- o **Importance**

  NEDs are vital for providing unbiased oversight, ensuring that the board's decisions are balanced and aligned with long-term goals.

- o **Example:**

  Cheryl Bachelder, as a non-executive director, played a significant role in steering governance reforms at Chick-fil-A, emphasising ethical decision-making and long-term value creation.

3. **Independent Directors**

Independent directors are a subset of non-executive directors who have no material or pecuniary relationships with the company, ensuring unbiased judgement.

- ○ **Roles and Responsibilities**

  - Providing impartial advice and oversight.
  - Strengthening the board's independence from management.
  - Chairing critical committees like audit, risk, and nomination.

- ○ **Importance**

  Independent directors enhance the board's credibility and accountability by minimising conflicts of interest.

- ○ **Example:**

  At Tata Group, the inclusion of independent directors helped stabilise governance during a leadership crisis, demonstrating their critical role in maintaining trust and transparency.

Board Director Roles

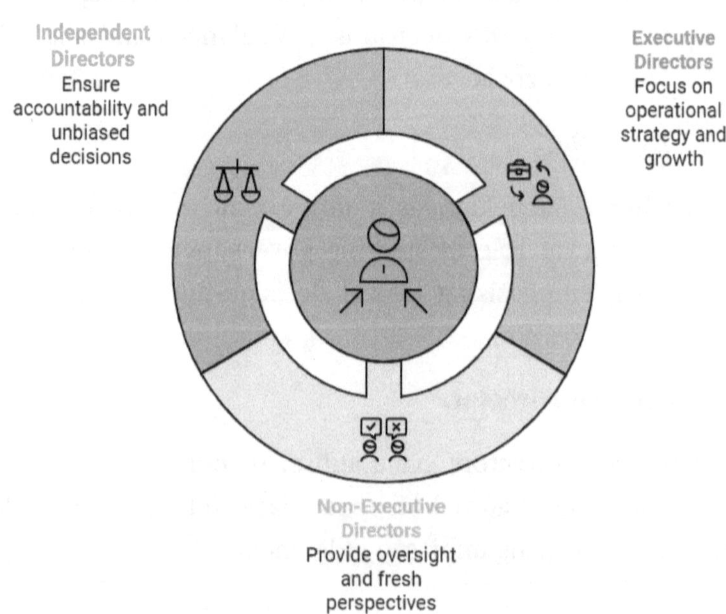

Practical Tips and Best Practices for Directors

1. **For Executive Directors**

   - Clearly separate board duties from operational roles to avoid micromanagement.
   - Foster open communication with the board to ensure alignment on key priorities.

2. **For Non-Executive Directors**

   - Stay informed about the business and industry trends to offer meaningful insights.
   - Build strong relationships with executive directors while maintaining independence.

3. **For Independent Directors**

   - Conduct thorough due diligence before accepting appointments.
   - Actively participate in committee work to ensure comprehensive oversight.

4. **For Boards as a Whole**

   - Ensure diversity in director types to create a balanced and dynamic boardroom.
   - Regularly review board composition to address evolving business needs.

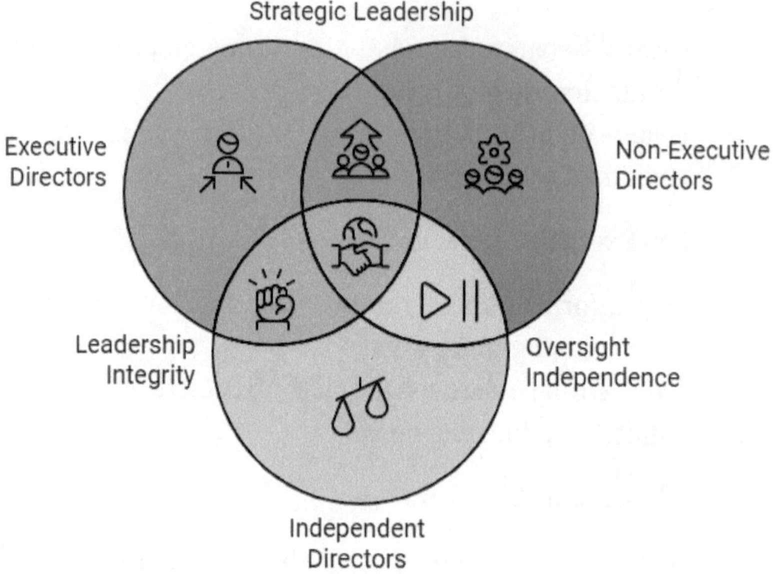

Interactive Element: Director Role Assessment

Checklist: Evaluating Director Effectiveness

1. Does the board have an adequate balance of executive, non-executive, and independent directors?
2. Are independent directors free from conflicts of interest?
3. Do non-executive directors actively challenge and support management?
4. Are executive directors providing transparent reports on operational performance?
5. Is the board regularly reviewing and updating its governance practices?

Discussion Question:

How can a board ensure that all director types collaborate effectively without overstepping their boundaries?

Key Takeaways

1. A balanced board composition is crucial for effective governance and long-term success.
2. Each type of director brings unique strengths, but collaboration and clear role definitions are essential.
3. Practical steps, such as regular evaluations and diverse appointments, can enhance board effectiveness.
4. Learning from historical and real-world examples can guide directors in their roles.

By understanding and leveraging the contributions of different director types, boards can build resilient governance structures capable of navigating complex challenges and driving sustainable growth.

Chapter 4

The Board's Relationship with Management

The relationship between a board and executive management is one of the most critical dynamics in corporate governance. A productive, balanced and transparent interaction ensures that the company's strategic vision is realised, risks are mitigated and shareholder value is maximised. Conversely, a dysfunctional relationship can lead to micromanagement, strategic paralysis or even governance failures that erode trust and damage the company's reputation.

This chapter explores how directors can navigate the fine line between providing oversight and enabling management autonomy. We delve into historical examples, practical advice, and tools to help directors foster a constructive partnership with management.

Example: The Case of Apple Inc. and Steve Jobs

In 1997, Apple was on the brink of collapse. The board of directors brought Steve Jobs back into the fold to turn the company around. While Jobs was undoubtedly a visionary, his relationship with the board required a delicate balance of trust and oversight.

Initially, the board gave Jobs broad autonomy to restructure the company, recognising his strategic insight. However, they also instituted mechanisms to monitor progress, such as quarterly performance reviews and milestone-based incentives. The collaboration worked seamlessly because both parties respected their roles—Jobs focused on innovation and execution, while the board ensured strategic alignment and financial accountability.

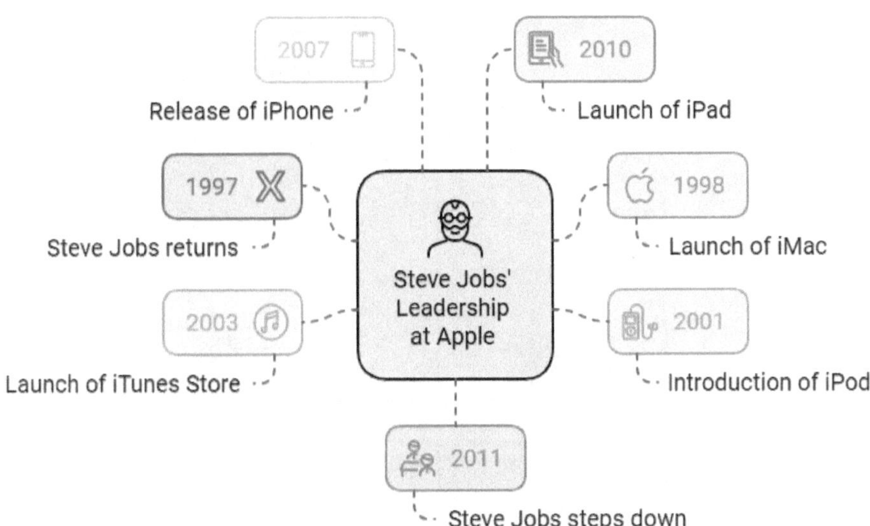

Contrast this with the situation at Enron in the early 2000s, where the board failed in its oversight duties. By allowing management to operate unchecked, critical risks and fraudulent practices went unnoticed until it was too late, resulting in one of the largest corporate collapses in history.

These contrasting examples underline the importance of striking the right balance between oversight and empowerment.

Practical Tips for Directors

1. **Establish Clear Boundaries and Roles**

   - **Oversight vs. Management:** Directors should focus on strategy, governance, and risk management rather than operational details.
   - Use a "policy governance model" to delineate board responsibilities from those of management.

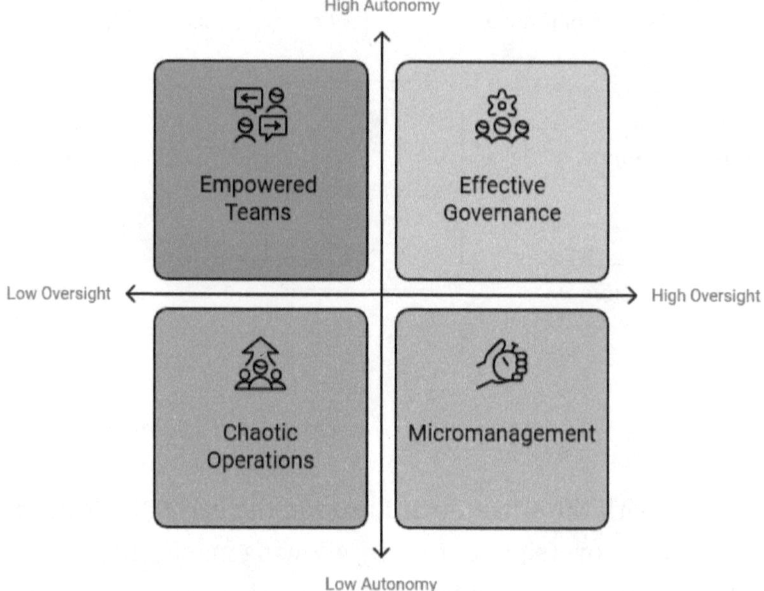

2. Build a Foundation of Trust

- Foster open communication channels with management.
- Encourage transparency by setting expectations for reporting and disclosures.

3. Regular Performance Evaluations

- Conduct periodic reviews of both CEO and board performance.
- Use key performance indicators (KPIs) tied to strategic goals to evaluate progress.

4. Support Management Decision-Making

- Provide a sounding board for key initiatives without undermining managerial authority.
- Leverage directors' diverse expertise to offer constructive advice.

5. **Avoid Common Pitfalls**

- **Micromanagement:** Interfering in day-to-day operations can demotivate management and blur lines of accountability.
- **Rubber-Stamping:** Approving management's proposals without adequate scrutiny undermines governance.

Challenge	Impact	Solution
Lack of communication	Mistrust and misalignment	Regular meetings and clear reporting
Board overstepping	Demotivated management	Role clarity and trust-building exercises
Rubber-stamping decisions	Poor strategic outcomes	Encourage critical discussions
Lack of performance metrics	Difficulty in evaluation	Establish KPIs and dashboards

Interactive Element: Checklist for Evaluating Board-Management Relations

Use this checklist to assess the health of your board's relationship with management:

1. Are roles and responsibilities clearly defined?
2. Is there mutual respect and trust between the board and executive team?
3. Are management reports clear, comprehensive, and timely?
4. Does the board provide constructive feedback without overstepping boundaries?
5. Are executive compensation and incentives aligned with long-term company goals?

Key Takeaways

1. **Trust and Role Clarity:** A strong board-management relationship is built on trust and a clear understanding of roles and responsibilities.

2. **Constructive Oversight:** Directors should focus on governance and strategy while supporting, not undermining, management autonomy.
3. **Continuous Evaluation:** Regular performance reviews for both management and the board ensure accountability and alignment with corporate goals.
4. **Learning from Examples:** Historical successes and failures, like Apple and Enron, highlight the importance of balance in this relationship.

Discussion Question:

What strategies would you employ to rebuild trust between the board and management after a conflict or governance failure? Discuss specific steps that balance accountability with partnership.

Chapter 5

The Board's Relationship with Shareholders

Shareholders are the lifeblood of any corporation. Their investment provides the capital that fuels innovation, growth, and operational sustainability. The board of directors serves as the bridge between shareholders and the company, ensuring their interests are protected while fostering sustainable business practices.

The relationship between the board and shareholders is central to corporate governance, rooted in fiduciary duties of care, loyalty, and good faith. Directors must navigate the complexities of balancing short-term shareholder expectations with long-term company goals. This chapter delves into the nuances of this critical relationship, offering historical insights, practical advice, and tools for effective engagement.

Example: Unilever and the Shareholder Revolt of 2018

In 2018, consumer goods giant Unilever proposed consolidating its headquarters in the Netherlands, a move seen as a way to shield itself from potential hostile takeovers. The decision, while strategically sound for management, sparked outrage among UK shareholders. It would have resulted in Unilever's exclusion from the FTSE 100 index, forcing many UK-based funds to sell their shares.

The board faced intense scrutiny from investors who accused them of prioritising management convenience over shareholder interests. After months of engagement with investors, including town halls, individual meetings, and public disclosures, the board ultimately reversed its decision.

This incident highlights the delicate balance boards must maintain—listening to shareholders while ensuring decisions align with the company's strategic vision. The board's willingness to engage openly with shareholders and reconsider its stance exemplifies effective shareholder relations under pressure.

Practical Tips for Directors

1. Understand Fiduciary Duties

- **Duty of Care:** Make informed decisions based on thorough research and expert advice.
- **Duty of Loyalty:** Avoid conflicts of interest and prioritise shareholder interests above personal or management agendas.
- **Duty of Good Faith:** Act in the best interest of the company with honesty and integrity.

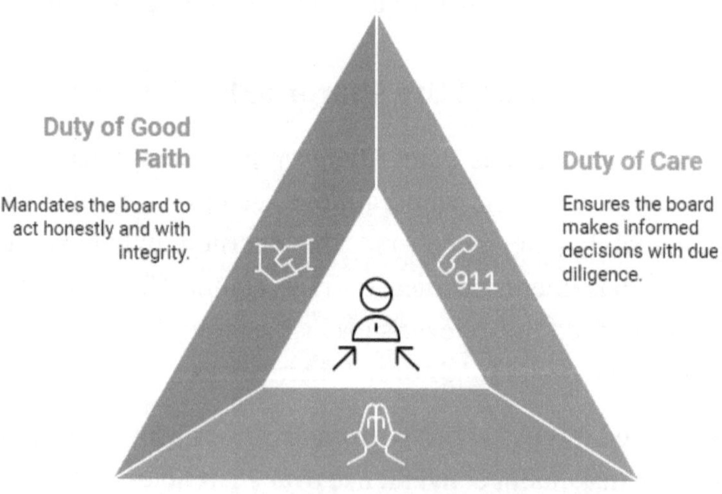

2. Foster Open Communication

- Regularly update shareholders on financial performance, strategic initiatives, and risks through annual reports, earnings calls, and shareholder meetings.
- Encourage dialogue by providing multiple channels for feedback, such as surveys or investor relations teams.

3. Balance Interests

- Address the needs of different shareholder groups: institutional investors, retail shareholders, and activists.
- Strive to align short-term profitability with long-term growth to satisfy varied investor priorities.

4. Engage with Activist Shareholders

- **Proactive Engagement:** Identify activist concerns early and address them transparently.
- **Negotiation Over Confrontation:** Seek collaborative solutions rather than adversarial stances.

5. Use Shareholder Votes Wisely

- Treat shareholder voting as a tool for empowerment, not just compliance.
- Ensure that votes on key issues such as executive compensation, mergers, or strategic shifts are well-informed and reflective of shareholder preferences.

Table: Shareholder Types and Engagement Strategies

Type of Shareholder	Primary Concern	Engagement Strategy
Institutional Investors	Long-term returns	Regular performance reviews and meetings
Retail Shareholders	Dividends and stability	Simple, clear communication and surveys
Activist Investors	Strategic changes	Open dialogue, responsiveness, and transparency

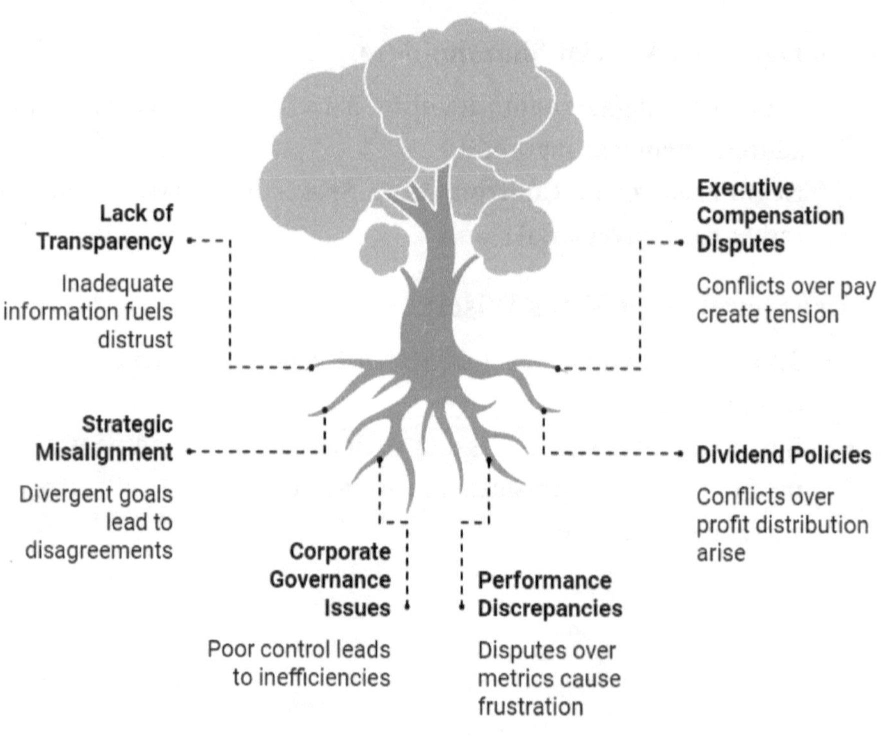

Interactive Element: Shareholder Engagement Checklist

Use this checklist to evaluate your board's effectiveness in managing shareholder relations:

1. Are all shareholder communications clear, timely, and comprehensive?
2. Does the board understand the priorities of major shareholder groups?
3. Are mechanisms in place for shareholders to voice concerns and provide feedback?
4. Has the board established a process to manage conflicts between short-term and long-term interests?
5. Does the company have a clear strategy to address activist shareholders?

Discussion Question:

Consider a scenario where a board decides to cut dividends temporarily to reinvest in a strategic growth initiative. Shareholders are upset. How should the board communicate this decision to ensure understanding and support?

Key Takeaways

1. **Fiduciary Duties are Paramount:** The board's primary responsibility is to safeguard shareholder interests through care, loyalty, and good faith.
2. **Communication is Key:** Transparent, proactive, and regular engagement builds trust with shareholders.
3. **Balancing Act:** Effective directors balance the sometimes conflicting priorities of short-term shareholder expectations and long-term corporate growth.
4. **Preparedness Matters:** Understanding shareholder dynamics and having a strategy to manage activists or conflicts ensures smoother relations.

5. **Learning from Experience:** Case studies like Unilever demonstrate the importance of listening to shareholder feedback while maintaining strategic direction.

By mastering the art of shareholder engagement, directors can enhance trust, align on goals, and foster a relationship that drives sustainable success for all stakeholders.

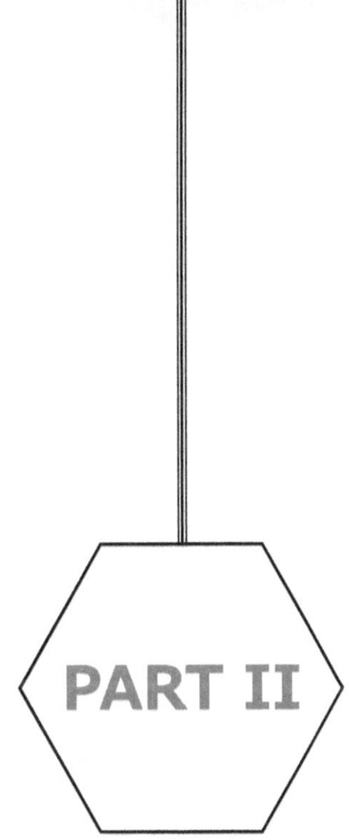

Board Composition and Structure

Chapter 6

Board Composition

Why Board Composition Matters

Board composition is one of the most critical elements in corporate governance. It determines not only the strategic direction of a company but also its ability to navigate challenges, foster innovation, and maintain trust with stakeholders. An effective board balances diverse skills, experiences, and perspectives to make informed decisions and address complex business issues.

However, a poorly composed board can lead to groupthink, lack of oversight, and ineffective governance. For example, during the 2008 financial crisis, several corporate boards were criticised for lacking financial expertise and independence, leading to inadequate risk management. By contrast, companies with well-structured boards were better equipped to weather the storm.

This chapter delves into the key factors shaping board composition, explores lessons from historical and contemporary examples, and provides practical guidance for creating a balanced, effective board.

Example: Board Composition in Action

In the years leading up to its collapse, Lehman Brothers' board was criticised for its lack of diversity in expertise. The board had several directors with limited financial or risk management backgrounds, despite the company's exposure to high-risk investments. This imbalance resulted in poor oversight of critical decisions and an inability to challenge management effectively.

Contrast this with the example of Unilever, whose board composition is widely regarded as a benchmark for effective governance. The company emphasises a diverse mix of skills, including sustainability expertise, financial acumen, and international experience. This diversity has enabled Unilever to innovate and maintain resilience, even in challenging market conditions.

The contrasting outcomes of these two boards underscore the importance of aligning board composition with a company's strategic needs.

Key Factors Influencing Board Composition

1. **Board Size**

   Optimal board size varies by organisation but typically ranges from 5 to 15. A smaller board facilitates quicker decision-making, while a larger board offers broader expertise.

   - **Example**: Tesla's board has been criticised for being too small to provide sufficient oversight, while General Electric's historically large board faced challenges in aligning diverse opinions.

2. **Diversity**

   Diversity encompasses gender, ethnicity, professional background, and global perspectives. Diverse boards are better equipped to understand varied stakeholder needs and foster innovation.

   - **Example**: In 2021, Nasdaq introduced rules requiring listed companies to have at least one female director and one from an underrepresented group, recognising the value of diversity.

3. **Skillsets and Expertise**

   Boards should include directors with expertise in finance, technology, marketing, legal matters, and sustainability to address multifaceted business challenges.

- **Example**: Apple's board includes technology and design experts, reflecting its innovation-driven strategy.

4. **Independence**

Independent directors play a crucial role in unbiased decision-making and risk management. Best practices recommend that a majority of the board be independent.

- **Example**: Google's parent company, Alphabet, maintains a majority of independent directors to strengthen governance.

5. **Tenure and Refreshment**

Balanced tenure ensures continuity without stagnation. Long-tenured directors bring institutional knowledge, while new members offer fresh perspectives.

- **Example**: Exxon Mobil faced shareholder pressure in 2021 to refresh its board, ultimately appointing directors with climate expertise.

Table: Factors Determining Board Composition

Factor	Key Considerations	Examples
Size	Small vs. large boards	Tesla (small), GE (large)
Diversity	Gender, ethnicity, background, global view	Nasdaq diversity rules
Skillsets	Finance, technology, legal, ESG	Apple's technology-focused board
Independence	Majority independent directors	Alphabet's independent board
Tenure	Balanced refreshment and continuity	ExxonMobil's board refreshment efforts

Practical Tips and Best Practices

1. **Conduct Regular Board Evaluations**

   Assess the board's performance and composition annually to identify skill gaps and areas for improvement.

2. **Align Composition with Strategy**

   Ensure that board expertise aligns with the company's strategic priorities, such as technology, sustainability, or global expansion.

3. **Prioritise Diversity and Inclusion**

   Establish policies to attract diverse candidates and set measurable diversity goals.

4. **Limit Over Boarding**

   Directors serving on multiple boards may struggle to dedicate sufficient time and attention. Limit over boarding to enhance focus.

5. **Leverage Board Committees**

   Use specialised committees (e.g., audit, risk, and nomination) to deepen oversight and focus on critical areas.

6. **Encourage Continuous Learning**

   Provide directors with training on emerging issues, such as cybersecurity, ESG (environmental, social, and governance) risks, and artificial intelligence (AI).

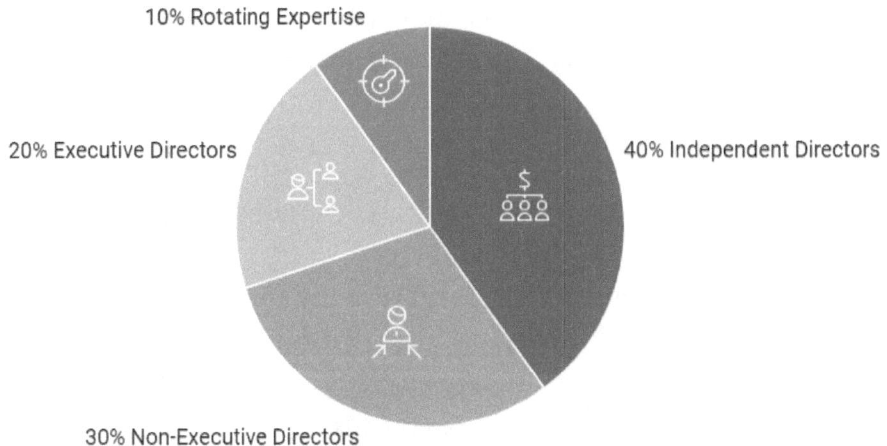

Criteria	Effective Boards	Ineffective Boards
Diversity	Balanced representation	Homogeneous composition
Expertise	Varied skillsets	Limited expertise
Independence	Strong oversight	Weak accountability
Refreshment Policies	Regular updates	Stagnant composition

Interactive Element: Board Composition Checklist

Checklist: Evaluating Your Board's Composition

1. Does the board size align with the organisation's complexity and strategic needs?
2. Is there a diverse mix of skills, backgrounds, and perspectives?
3. Do independent directors constitute a majority of the board?
4. Are there policies in place for regular board refreshment?
5. Does the board include members with expertise in critical areas like finance, technology, and ESG?
6. Is the board actively pursuing gender and ethnic diversity?
7. Are directors provided with training and development opportunities?

Discussion Question:

How can boards balance the need for expertise with the imperative of diversity, especially in rapidly evolving industries?

Key Takeaways

1. Board composition is a critical determinant of governance effectiveness and long-term success.
2. Factors like size, diversity, expertise, independence, and tenure play pivotal roles in shaping board dynamics.
3. Historical and contemporary examples demonstrate the impact of balanced versus imbalanced boards.
4. Practical steps, including regular evaluations and diversity policies, can optimise board composition.
5. A well-composed board fosters innovation, accountability, and resilience, enabling organisations to thrive in complex environments.

By understanding and applying these principles, directors can build and maintain boards that drive sustainable value creation and strong corporate governance.

Chapter 7

Board Committees

The Pillars of Effective Governance

Board committees are the specialised arms of corporate governance, enabling boards to manage complex responsibilities effectively. By delegating specific tasks to committees like audit, compensation, and nominating committees, boards can focus on strategic oversight while ensuring detailed attention to critical areas.

The relevance of board committees lies in their ability to enhance governance by promoting transparency, accountability, and specialisation. Committees offer a structured way to address areas like financial reporting, executive remuneration, and board succession planning. When functioning effectively, they strengthen trust among stakeholders and improve overall board performance.

In contrast, ineffective committee work can lead to governance failures, as demonstrated in several corporate crises where audit or compensation committees failed to detect or mitigate risks. This chapter explores the roles and responsibilities of key committees, real-world examples, and practical guidance for directors.

Example: Strengthening Governance Through Committees

Case Study: General Electric (GE)

In the early 2000s, GE faced criticism for its lack of oversight and transparency, especially in financial reporting. The company revamped its board structure, focusing on strengthening its audit committee. By appointing directors with strong financial expertise and implementing rigorous internal controls, GE's audit committee restored stakeholder confidence.

The audit committee's role was instrumental during the 2008 financial crisis when GE managed to navigate challenging times through sound financial governance. This example highlights how a robust committee structure can mitigate risks and foster resilience in turbulent times.

Key Board Committees

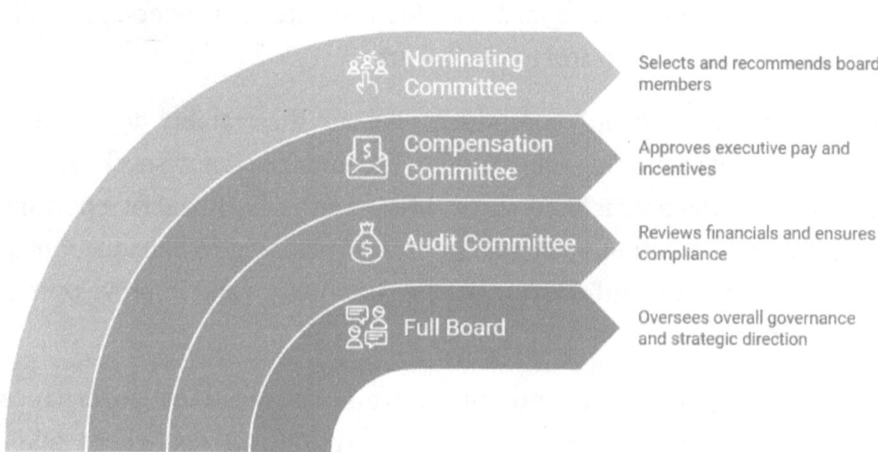

1. **Audit Committee**

    o   **Role and Responsibilities**

        - Oversee financial reporting and disclosures.
        - Ensure compliance with laws, regulations, and internal policies.
        - Monitor internal controls and risk management systems.
        - Engage with external and internal auditors.

- o **Example:**

  The audit committee of JP Morgan Chase played a pivotal role in uncovering and addressing the "London Whale" trading loss in 2012, showcasing the importance of diligent oversight.

- o **Best Practices**

  - Include members with financial expertise.
  - Maintain independence to avoid conflicts of interest.

2. **Compensation (or Remuneration) Committee**

   - o **Role and Responsibilities**

     - Determine executive remuneration policies and packages.
     - Align compensation with performance and shareholder interests.
     - Monitor equity-based compensation plans, such as stock options.

   - o **Example:**

     Apple's compensation committee structured a pay package for CEO Tim Cook that tied a significant portion of his remuneration to performance metrics, aligning his interests with those of shareholders.

   - o **Best Practices**

     - Regularly review and benchmark compensation policies.
     - Ensure transparency in reporting executive pay.

3. **Nominating (or Governance) Committee**

   - o **Role and Responsibilities**

     - Oversee board composition and succession planning.

- Identify and recommend director candidates.
- Evaluate board performance and recommend improvements.

○ **Example:**

Microsoft's nominating committee played a key role in the seamless transition from Steve Ballmer to Satya Nadella, ensuring continuity and strategic alignment.

○ **Best Practices**

- Focus on diversity and expertise in board appointments.
- Conduct regular evaluations to identify gaps in board skills.

Table: Roles and Responsibilities of Key Committees

Committee	Key Focus Areas	Example Contributions
Audit	Financial reporting, risk management	Addressing the "London Whale" incident
Compensation	Executive pay, performance alignment	Structuring Tim Cook's pay package
Nominating	Board succession, diversity	Microsoft's CEO transition

Practical Tips and Best Practices

1. **General Tips for All Committees**

   ○ Clearly define roles and responsibilities in committee charters.
   ○ Foster open communication between committees and the full board.
   ○ Conduct regular self-assessments to evaluate committee effectiveness.

2. **For Audit Committees**

    o   Stay updated on changes in accounting standards and regulations.
    o   Ensure robust whistleblower mechanisms to detect fraud.

3. **For Compensation Committees**

    o   Avoid excessive executive pay by tying rewards to long-term performance.
    o   Engage with shareholders to address concerns about remuneration policies.

4. **For Nominating Committees**

    o   Develop a robust succession planning framework.
    o   Use external search firms to identify diverse candidates.

Table: Effective vs. Ineffective Committees

Criteria	Effective Committees	Ineffective Committees
Independence	Majority independent	Conflicted members
Expertise	Relevant skills present	Lack of specialized knowledge
Communication	Regular and transparent	Infrequent or unclear reports

Interactive Element: Committee Effectiveness Checklist

Checklist: Assessing the Strength of Your Board Committees

1. Does each committee have a clearly defined charter?
2. Are committee members independent and appropriately skilled?
3. Does the audit committee include at least one financial expert?
4. Is the compensation committee aligning executive pay with company performance?
5. Does the nominating committee prioritise diversity and expertise in board appointments?

6. Are there regular assessments of committee performance and effectiveness?
7. Do committees have access to the resources they need to perform their duties?

Discussion Question:

How can committees balance their focus on oversight with the need to support management in achieving strategic goals?

Key Takeaways

1. Board committees are essential for managing the increasing complexity of governance responsibilities.
2. The audit, compensation, and nominating committees play pivotal roles in financial oversight, executive remuneration, and board composition.
3. Real-world examples demonstrate how effective committee work can strengthen governance, while failures highlight the risks of inadequate oversight.
4. Practical steps, such as clear charters and regular evaluations, can enhance committee performance.
5. Collaboration between committees and the full board is crucial for strategic alignment and decision-making.

By leveraging the strengths of specialised committees, boards can improve governance standards, foster transparency, and build long-term value for stakeholders.

Chapter 8

Board Leadership

Effective board leadership is essential for the success of any organisation. It ensures the board operates cohesively, makes informed decisions, and fulfils its governance responsibilities. A well-led board fosters trust, encourages diverse viewpoints, and supports management in achieving the company's strategic goals.

The distinct roles of the **Chair**, **CEO**, and **Lead Independent Director (LID)** create a dynamic interplay that shapes the board's effectiveness. Each role has unique responsibilities that must align to prevent conflicts, enhance accountability, and drive corporate performance. This chapter explores these roles in detail, providing insights into how leadership impacts governance and offering practical guidance for directors.

Example: Wells Fargo's Leadership and Governance Overhaul

Wells Fargo provides a compelling example of how board leadership roles can influence governance, especially during a crisis. The company faced a significant reputational and operational crisis in 2016 when it was revealed that employees had created millions of unauthorised customer accounts to meet aggressive sales targets. This scandal exposed serious flaws in Wells Fargo's governance and leadership structure, raising questions about the board's ability to provide adequate oversight and challenge management.

Governance Challenges:

At the time, John Stumpf held the dual roles of CEO and chair of the board, which concentrated power and diminished the board's independence. The lack of a strong Lead Independent Director (LID) further reduced the board's ability to provide checks and balances. As a result, the board was criticised for failing to recognise and address the systemic issues that allowed unethical practices to flourish.

Leadership Restructuring

In the wake of the scandal, Wells Fargo's board implemented significant changes to rebuild trust and enhance governance:

1. **Separation of CEO and Chair Roles:**

    Stumpf resigned, and the board separated the roles of CEO and chair to improve accountability and oversight. This restructuring ensured that the board chair could independently lead the board without conflicts of interest.

2. **Appointment of a Lead Independent Director:**

   Wells Fargo strengthened its governance by appointing a strong LID, who played a critical role in facilitating independent discussions, acting as a liaison between the board and management, and ensuring the board's oversight functions were robust.

3. **Renewed Focus on Board Composition:**

   The board underwent significant changes, bringing in directors with expertise in risk management, compliance, and ethics to address the shortcomings revealed during the crisis.

4. **Cultural Reforms and Oversight:**

   The new leadership structure allowed the board to work closely with management on cultural reforms, including revising incentive structures to prioritise ethical behaviour over aggressive sales targets.

Role	Primary Responsibility	Supporting Actions
Chair	Board leadership	Setting agendas, managing conflicts
CEO	Organizational management	Implementing strategy, reporting to the board
Lead Independent Director	Oversight and shareholder engagement	Acting as a liaison, ensuring independence

Outcomes and Lessons for Boards:

Wells Fargo's overhaul of its leadership structure marked a critical step in regaining stakeholder trust and strengthening governance. By clearly delineating the roles of the CEO, chair, and LID, the board was better equipped to provide independent oversight, challenge management, and prioritise ethical conduct.

This case highlights several key takeaways for boards:

- **Independence Matters:** Clear separation of leadership roles fosters accountability and mitigates conflicts of interest.
- **Strengthen Board Dynamics:** A strong LID ensures that independent directors have a voice and that board discussions remain balanced.
- **Focus on Board Composition:** Regular refreshment of board skills and expertise is essential, especially during or after a crisis.
- **Cultural Oversight:** Board leadership must prioritise ethical behaviour and align corporate culture with governance principles.

The Wells Fargo example underscores the importance of effective board leadership in navigating crises and driving governance improvements that safeguard an organisation's integrity and long-term success.

Practical Tips for Directors

1. **The Role of the Chair**

   - **Primary Responsibilities:** The chair leads the board, sets agendas, facilitates discussions, and ensures directors fulfil their governance duties.
   - **Key Skills:** Strong communication, neutrality, and the ability to mediate conflicts.
   - **Best Practices:**
     - Regularly evaluate the board's performance and address gaps.
     - Foster an environment where all directors feel comfortable sharing their perspectives.

2. **The Role of the CEO**

   - **Primary Responsibilities:** The CEO manages the organisation's day-to-day operations and executes the board's strategic vision.

- **Key Skills:** Leadership, strategic thinking, and operational expertise.
- **Best Practices:**

  - Maintain open communication with the chair and the board.
  - Provide timely and accurate updates on organisational performance.

3. **The Role of the Lead Independent Director (LID)**

- **Primary Responsibilities:** The LID acts as a counterbalance, particularly in boards where the chair and CEO roles are combined. They serve as an intermediary between the chair and other directors.
- **Key Skills:** Independence, objectivity, and the ability to foster consensus.
- **Best Practices:**

  - Engage directly with shareholders on governance issues.
  - Provide feedback to the chair and CEO to improve board dynamics.

4. **Ensuring Role Clarity**

- Clearly define each role's responsibilities in the Board Charter.
- Regularly review and update governance policies to reflect evolving organisational needs.

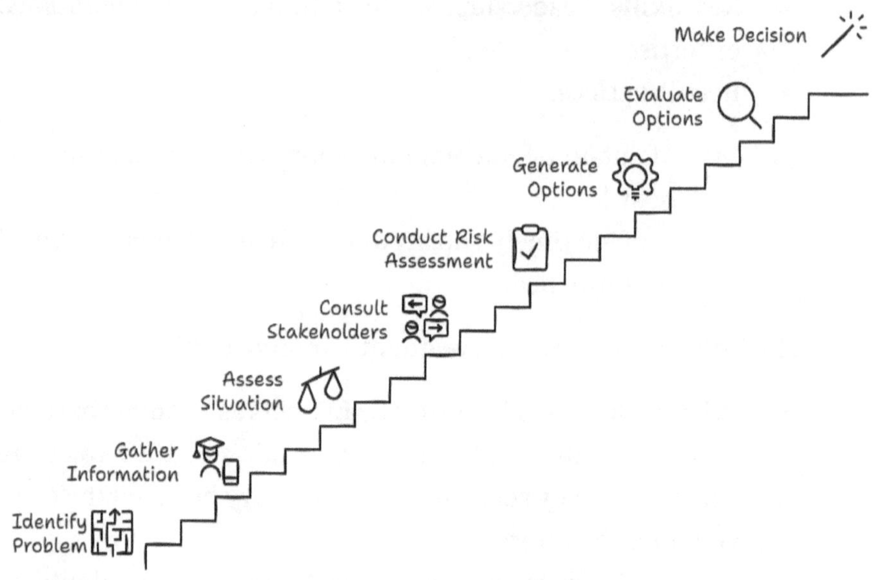

Interactive Element: Board Leadership Checklist

Evaluate your board leadership using this checklist:

1. Are the roles of the chair, CEO, and LID clearly defined and documented?
2. Does the chair facilitate productive and inclusive board discussions?
3. Is there a constructive working relationship between the chair and CEO?
4. Does the LID provide effective oversight and feedback to leadership?
5. Are leadership roles reviewed regularly to ensure alignment with governance best practices?

Discussion Question:

In a scenario where the CEO and chair are the same person, what steps can the Lead Independent Director take to ensure the board's independence and effectiveness? Discuss strategies and potential challenges.

Key Takeaways

1. **Distinct Roles are Critical:** Clear delineation of responsibilities among the chair, CEO, and LID prevents conflicts and promotes accountability.
2. **Leadership Shapes Governance:** Strong board leadership enhances decision-making, fosters trust, and ensures effective oversight.
3. **Adaptability is Key:** Leadership roles should evolve to meet the organisation's changing needs and governance challenges.
4. **Learning from Failures:** Cases like Boeing highlight the risks of poorly defined leadership roles and the value of restructuring for improved governance.
5. **Continuous Evaluation:** Boards must regularly assess the effectiveness of their leadership structure to maintain alignment with best practices.

Board leadership is the cornerstone of effective governance. By understanding and refining the roles of the chair, CEO, and Lead Independent Director, boards can navigate challenges and drive their organisations toward long-term success.

Chapter 9

Board Diversity and Inclusion

Board diversity and inclusion (D&I) are no longer optional – they are essential for effective governance, better decision-making, and sustainable success. Diversity on boards encompasses a range of attributes, including gender, ethnicity, age, professional background, skills, and experiences. Inclusion ensures these diverse perspectives are valued, leading to better group dynamics and innovative solutions.

Studies consistently show that diverse boards outperform their homogeneous counterparts. For example, a McKinsey report found that companies in the top quartile for board diversity were 35% more likely to have financial returns above their industry medians. However, many boards still face challenges in achieving meaningful diversity and fostering an inclusive environment.

This chapter explores the critical role of D&I in corporate governance, highlights real-world examples, and offers actionable strategies to build diverse and inclusive boards.

Example: Nasdaq's Push for Diversity in 2020

In December 2020, Nasdaq proposed new listing rules requiring companies to have at least one woman and one underrepresented minority or LGBTQ+ individual on their boards – or explain why they do not. This landmark proposal marked the first time a stock exchange linked board diversity to corporate performance.

While some companies initially resisted the change, many embraced the opportunity to improve their boards. One notable success story is Zendesk, a tech company that overhauled its board composition, adding directors from varied ethnic backgrounds and professional experiences. This shift brought fresh perspectives and aligned the company's governance with its diverse customer base.

The Nasdaq initiative sparked a broader conversation about diversity's importance, with ripple effects across industries and geographies. It highlighted how external pressures and internal leadership commitment could drive systemic change.

Practical Tips for Directors

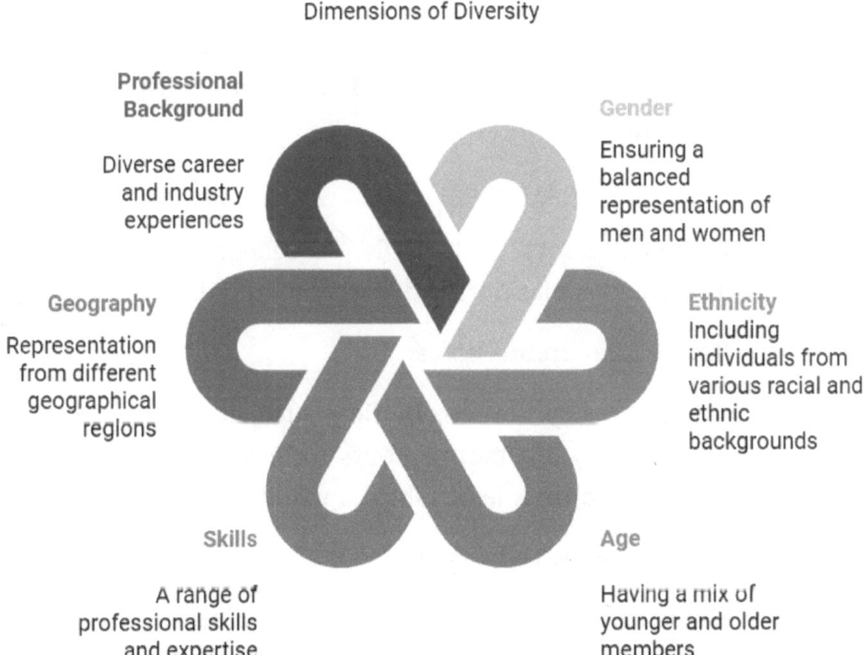

1. **Building a Diverse Board**

    •   **Expand Recruitment Pipelines:**

        Partner with organisations specialising in underrepresented talent, such as Women on Boards or The Board Challenge.

- **Use Skills-Based Criteria:**

  Focus on competencies rather than traditional qualifications to attract candidates with unconventional but valuable experiences.

- **Think Beyond Tokenism:**

  Diversity should be substantive, not symbolic. Aim for meaningful representation across multiple dimensions.

2. **Fostering Inclusion**

   - **Create an Inclusive Culture:**

     Ensure every board member feels valued and empowered to contribute. Foster open dialogue and respect diverse opinions.

   - **Provide Bias Training:**

     Equip directors with tools to recognise and mitigate unconscious bias during discussions and decision-making.

   - **Rotate Leadership Roles:**

     Distribute key responsibilities, such as committee chair positions, to diverse members to leverage their strengths and develop their leadership capabilities.

3. **Monitor and Measure Progress**

   - Regularly assess board composition against diversity goals.
   - Use metrics such as gender balance, ethnic representation, and skill variety to track progress and identify gaps.

Interactive Element: Diversity and Inclusion Checklist

Evaluate your board's D&I efforts with this checklist:

1. Does the board composition reflect the organisation's customer base or stakeholder demographics?

2. Are recruitment strategies inclusive of underrepresented groups?
3. Is there a policy or commitment to diversity at the board level?
4. Are inclusive practices integrated into boardroom discussions?
5. Is progress in D&I tracked and reported transparently?

Discussion Question:

Imagine a board of a multinational company where diversity is limited to one gender and one ethnicity. What steps would you recommend to make the board more diverse and inclusive without disrupting its existing dynamics?

Key Takeaways

1. **Diversity Drives Success:** Diverse boards make better decisions, foster innovation, and align with stakeholder expectations.
2. **Inclusion is the Key:** Simply having diverse members is not enough; inclusion ensures every voice is heard and valued.
3. **Proactive Measures Work:** Recruiting from diverse pipelines, adopting inclusive practices, and monitoring progress are critical to achieving D&I goals.
4. **Learn from Success Stories:** Initiatives like Nasdaq's listing rules demonstrate how D&I can be institutionalised and lead to tangible benefits.
5. **A Continuous Journey:** Diversity and inclusion are not one-time efforts but ongoing commitments requiring board-level leadership.

By embracing diversity and fostering inclusion, boards can better navigate complex challenges, represent stakeholder interests, and drive long-term success.

Chapter 10

Board Succession Planning

The Imperative of Board Succession Planning

Board succession planning is one of the most critical yet often overlooked aspects of corporate governance. It ensures that a company is prepared for leadership transitions, whether planned or unexpected. Proper succession planning is vital for maintaining stability, securing long-term success, and fostering the continuity of vision and strategy within the organisation. For directors, it's crucial to understand that succession planning is not just about filling vacancies but about ensuring that the right leadership talent is in place at all times to meet the challenges of the future.

In an increasingly complex business world, where the pace of change accelerates, it is more important than ever for boards to have a structured, strategic approach to succession. Whether it's for the CEO, other senior executives, or even board members, the ability to navigate leadership changes seamlessly can make the difference between continued growth and disruption.

For companies that fail to plan ahead, leadership transitions can be disruptive, resulting in a loss of institutional knowledge, strategic misalignments, and even reputational damage. In contrast, well-executed succession planning facilitates a smooth transition, maintains investor confidence, and strengthens the company's position in the market.

Example: A Seamless Leadership Transition

Case Study: The Transition at Microsoft

One of the most notable examples of effective board succession planning is the leadership transition at Microsoft from Steve Ballmer to Satya Nadella. In 2014, when Ballmer announced his retirement, the board at Microsoft had already put in place a comprehensive succession plan.

The nominating committee had spent several years preparing for this moment, carefully evaluating both internal and external candidates. Nadella, who was an insider, had already demonstrated strong leadership within Microsoft, particularly through his work leading the cloud division.

What made this transition especially smooth was not just the appointment of Nadella, but the process that surrounded it. The board had communicated openly with key stakeholders, including employees, investors, and analysts, about the decision-making process. They ensured continuity in leadership while introducing fresh perspectives, striking the delicate balance between stability and innovation.

The successful leadership transition was credited with revitalising Microsoft, as Nadella shifted the company's focus to cloud computing and artificial intelligence, driving significant growth. This is a prime example of how strategic succession planning can set the stage for a new phase of corporate success.

Key Steps in Effective Board Succession Planning

1. **Assess the Current and Future Needs of the Board**

   Succession planning begins with understanding the company's strategic direction and the skills required at the board level. Directors must assess whether the current board composition is equipped to meet future challenges. This includes identifying gaps in skills, expertise, and diversity.

- o   *Actionable Tip*: Conduct a board skills audit to identify areas where additional expertise or diversity may be needed.

2. **Define the Role of the Board Member or Executive Being Replaced**

Whether the transition is for a director or a senior executive, it is crucial to define the role clearly. This involves understanding the responsibilities, expectations, and long-term goals associated with the position. The board must ensure that the individual stepping into the role is not only qualified but also aligned with the company's values and vision.

- o   *Actionable Tip*: Create detailed role descriptions and performance expectations for all key positions.

3. **Develop a Talent Pipeline**

An effective succession plan includes identifying and grooming potential candidates ahead of time. The talent pipeline should consist of both internal and external candidates. Internal candidates should be given the opportunity to develop the skills and experience necessary to step into leadership roles, while external candidates can bring in fresh perspectives and ideas.

- o   *Actionable Tip*: Encourage cross-functional training and leadership development programmes to build internal leadership.

4. **Implement a Structured Succession Process**

The succession process should be formalised with clear timelines, communication strategies, and decision-making protocols. This ensures that when a vacancy arises, the transition is smooth, and there is no uncertainty about the process.

- *Actionable Tip*: Set up a formal committee for succession planning, with clearly defined roles for evaluating candidates.

5. **Ensure Transparency and Stakeholder Involvement**

Successful board succession planning involves communication with key stakeholders, such as shareholders, employees, and other senior executives. Transparency ensures that the process is viewed as credible and that there is broad support for the chosen successor.

- *Actionable Tip*: Keep open lines of communication with stakeholders and provide updates on the succession planning process.

6. **Focus on Diversity and Inclusion**

Board succession planning provides an excellent opportunity to focus on enhancing diversity at the board level. A diverse board brings varied perspectives, which can help the company navigate challenges and seize new opportunities.

- *Actionable Tip*: Implement diversity goals as part of the succession planning process, ensuring that the board reflects the diversity of the communities in which the company operates.

7. **Regularly Review and Update the Succession Plan**

Succession planning is not a one-time activity; it requires continuous review and adjustment. As the company's needs evolve, so should the succession plan.

- *Actionable Tip*: Review the succession plan at least annually and make adjustments based on the company's strategic goals and changes in the talent pool.

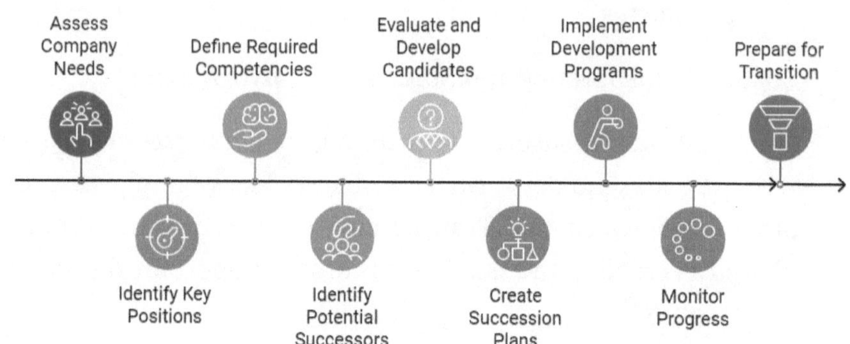

Practical Tips and Best Practices for Directors

1. **Anticipate Leadership Changes**

    Directors should work proactively to anticipate leadership changes rather than react when they occur. This means thinking about potential successors early and investing in their development.

2. **Engage with Internal and External Talent Pools**

    While it's important to have a pipeline of internal candidates, boards should also maintain relationships with external executives who could bring valuable experience to the company.

3. **Create a Transparent Process**

    A transparent and well-communicated succession process not only boosts confidence within the organisation but also with external stakeholders. Ensuring transparency in the selection process is key to securing buy-in from investors, employees, and other stakeholders.

4. **Ensure Continuity and Stability**

    When planning for leadership transitions, boards must aim for continuity in the company's strategic direction. Transitioning leadership shouldn't cause disruptions to the company's core values or strategic initiatives.

5. **Incorporate Succession Planning into Long-Term Strategy**

Succession planning should not be viewed as a standalone activity but integrated into the company's long-term strategic plan. Boards should align their succession strategies with the company's future direction and needs.

Interactive Element: Board Succession Planning Checklist

Table: Key Steps in Succession Planning and Their Importance

Step	Importance	Example Contribution
Conduct a skills audit	Identifies gaps in expertise and diversity	Ensures board has the right mix of skills
Define role responsibilities	Clarifies the expectations of the role	Prevents misalignment during transitions
Build a talent pipeline	Develops internal candidates for leadership	Strengthens long-term organizational stability
Implement a structured process	Ensures the process is clear and fair	Enhances transparency and stakeholder confidence

Checklist: Steps to Successful Succession Planning

- Conduct a comprehensive board skills audit.
- Define the role and responsibilities of the position being replaced.
- Identify and develop internal candidates for succession.
- Establish a formal, transparent process for succession.
- Regularly review and update the succession plan.
- Ensure diversity and inclusion in the selection process.
- Communicate the process and outcomes to key stakeholders.

Discussion Question:

How can a company balance the need for leadership continuity with the desire to inject new ideas and innovation during a leadership transition?

Key Takeaways

1. Board succession planning is a crucial element of corporate governance, ensuring leadership continuity and alignment with strategic goals.
2. A successful succession plan is proactive, structured, and transparent, involving clear role definitions and the development of internal talent.
3. By planning for both internal and external candidates, and integrating diversity into the process, boards can enhance their long-term effectiveness and resilience.
4. Real-world examples, like Microsoft's smooth leadership transition, demonstrate the positive impact of well-executed succession planning.
5. Directors must regularly review and update the succession plan to align with evolving company needs and industry dynamics.

Effective board succession planning ensures a smooth transition of leadership, maintaining the stability of the organisation and securing its future success.

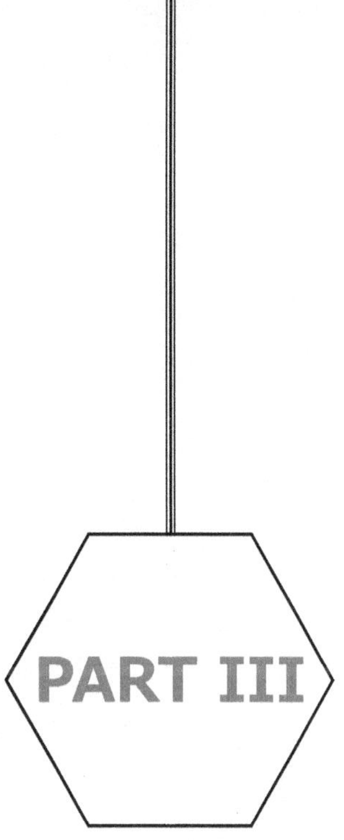

Corporate Governance Best Practices

Chapter 11

Corporate Governance Principles

Understanding Corporate Governance Principles

Corporate governance refers to the set of practices, principles, and rules that guide and govern the functioning of a company, particularly in relation to how it is directed and controlled. Effective corporate governance is foundational to creating trust with shareholders, employees, regulators, and the broader public, which directly impacts the company's ability to create long-term value. Directors, as stewards of the company, play a pivotal role in ensuring that governance principles are adhered to, as these principles are key to ensuring accountability, transparency, and ethical business practices.

At its core, corporate governance is about balancing the interests of various stakeholders, including shareholders, management, customers, suppliers, financiers, government, and the community. It aims to achieve organisational success by promoting an environment of fairness, responsibility, and transparency in decision-making processes.

Why is corporate governance important? In the modern era, characterised by increasing scrutiny and the potential for reputational risk, companies with robust governance frameworks are better positioned to build trust and avoid the risks of scandals, fraud, or mismanagement. Effective corporate governance enables better decision-making, enhances organisational accountability, and ultimately drives long-term business success.

Key frameworks such as the OECD (Organisation for Economic Co-operation and Development) Guidelines on Corporate Governance and the Cadbury Report have provided the foundation for modern governance structures. These frameworks emphasise the importance of accountability, transparency, responsibility, and fairness.

Example: The Enron Scandal

One of the most prominent cases in the history of corporate governance failure is the Enron scandal. Enron was once one of the largest energy companies in the world, with its stock prices reaching extraordinary heights. However, its downfall in 2001, attributed to widespread accounting fraud, exposed significant flaws in corporate governance.

Enron's leadership, under CEO Jeffrey Skilling and founder Kenneth Lay, engaged in fraudulent activities, including hiding debt and inflating profits through complex financial structures. The company's board, which should have provided oversight and direction, failed to challenge management's decisions or adequately supervise financial reporting practices.

What went wrong?

- **Lack of Independent Oversight**: The board lacked truly independent directors who could effectively challenge management's actions. Many of the directors had close relationships with the executives.
- **Failure of Transparency**: Financial statements were misleading, with off-balance-sheet entities masking liabilities.
- **Weak Audit Committees**: The audit committee failed to ask the right questions or ensure that external auditors (Arthur Andersen) were truly independent.
- **Ineffective Risk Management**: Enron's risk management practices were insufficient and not up to the level required to manage the complex financial instruments it created.

The Enron scandal ultimately led to the company's bankruptcy, the loss of thousands of jobs, and a significant erosion of trust in corporate America. The aftermath prompted major reforms in corporate governance, most notably the Sarbanes-Oxley Act, which sought to improve transparency, accountability, and corporate ethics.

Lesson Learned: Effective governance is essential to protecting against financial scandals. A board must have true independence, a culture of questioning management, and the ability to oversee financial practices with due diligence. The role of the audit committee and external auditors must not be underestimated in ensuring transparency and accuracy in financial reporting.

Key Principles of Corporate Governance

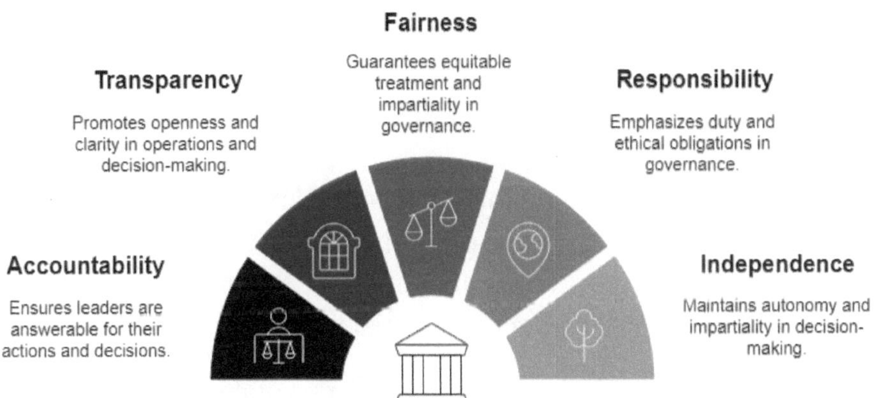

Corporate governance principles provide a structured framework to ensure that companies are managed in a way that promotes fairness, transparency, and accountability. The following principles are fundamental to good governance:

1. **Accountability**

    Accountability is the cornerstone of corporate governance. Directors must be held responsible for their actions and the company's performance. A strong accountability framework ensures that the board fulfils its obligations to shareholders and other stakeholders.

- o   *Best Practice*: Regular performance reviews of both individual directors and the board as a whole should be conducted to ensure they remain accountable.

2. **Transparency**

Transparency in corporate governance means that decisions are made with openness and clarity, and information is disclosed to stakeholders in a timely and comprehensive manner. Transparency prevents the manipulation of financial records and promotes trust among investors and the public.

- o   *Best Practice*: Companies should adhere to strict reporting and disclosure standards, providing shareholders with clear and accurate financial statements.

3. **Fairness**

Directors must ensure that all shareholders are treated equitably and that no group benefits at the expense of others. Fairness ensures that the interests of minority shareholders are protected and that all stakeholders are treated justly.

- o   *Best Practice*: Voting mechanisms should be transparent, and shareholders should have an opportunity to express their views on key decisions.

4. **Responsibility**

Directors must ensure that the company complies with legal and regulatory requirements and operates ethically. Responsibility includes considering the environmental, social, and governance (ESG) impact of business decisions.

    ◦ *Best Practice*: Corporate governance frameworks should include ESG considerations, and boards should ensure compliance with environmental and social governance standards.

5. **Independence**

An independent board, particularly through the use of independent directors, ensures that the decision-making process is unbiased and that management is appropriately monitored. Independence in the boardroom prevents conflicts of interest from influencing decisions.

    ◦ *Best Practice*: A majority of independent directors should sit on the board and key committees, such as the audit committee.

6. **Stakeholder Engagement**

Modern corporate governance emphasises not only the interests of shareholders but also the needs and concerns of other stakeholders, such as employees, customers, suppliers, and the broader community.

    ◦ *Best Practice*: Directors should ensure that there is open communication with all stakeholders and that their interests are considered in key decisions.

Practical Tips for Directors on Corporate Governance

1. **Create a Diverse Board**

Diversity, in terms of skills, experience, gender, and culture, strengthens the decision-making process. A variety of perspectives ensures that issues are approached from multiple angles and that the board is better equipped to tackle challenges.

- *Tip*: Actively seek diverse candidates for board positions, ensuring that diversity is prioritised as part of the board's strategic goals.

2. **Regularly Review Governance Frameworks**

Corporate governance principles and practices must evolve with changing regulations and market conditions. Boards should regularly review and update governance frameworks to ensure they remain relevant.

- *Tip*: Schedule annual reviews of governance structures and processes to ensure they align with the latest best practices and regulations.

3. **Foster a Culture of Open Dialogue**

A strong corporate governance framework encourages directors to openly question management, voice concerns, and engage in healthy debate. This approach fosters an environment of transparency and accountability.

- *Tip*: Encourage regular, candid discussions in board meetings, and ensure that dissenting opinions are heard and respected.

4. **Focus on Risk Management**

Directors should prioritise risk management to identify, assess, and mitigate potential risks to the company. A robust risk management framework is essential in maintaining business continuity.

- *Tip*: Ensure the board has access to real-time data on financial, operational, and reputational risks and regularly review risk management strategies.

5. **Ensure Effective Committees**

Corporate governance structures are often most effective when supported by specialised committees. The audit, compensation, and nomination committees play crucial roles in maintaining accountability, fairness, and independence.

- *Tip*: Ensure that key committees are properly staffed with independent directors and that they meet regularly to fulfil their duties.

Table: Examples of Corporate Governance Failures and Successes

Company	Type of Governance Failure	Lessons Learned
Enron	Fraudulent accounting practices, lack of independent oversight	Importance of independent board and financial transparency
Volkswagen	Emissions scandal, lack of board accountability	Need for accountability and stakeholder communication
Microsoft	Smooth leadership transition	Effective succession planning and transparent communication

Interactive Element: Corporate Governance Principles Quiz

Test your understanding of corporate governance principles with the following quiz:

1. Which of the following is NOT a key principle of corporate governance?

   a) Accountability
   b) Transparency
   c) Profit maximisation
   d) Independence

2. How can a company ensure fairness in decision-making?

   a) By ensuring all shareholders have an equal vote
   b) By giving management veto power
   c) By prioritising the interests of the majority shareholders
   d) By limiting communication with minority shareholders

3. What is the most effective way to foster transparency in corporate governance?

    a)   Keep financial information private
    b)   Regularly release inaccurate financial reports
    c)   Disclose financial reports in a timely and accurate manner
    d)   Focus only on the board's internal processes

Key Takeaways

1. Corporate governance principles are essential for building trust and ensuring the long-term success of a company.
2. Accountability, transparency, fairness, responsibility, and independence are the key principles that should guide a board's actions.
3. Governance failures, like the Enron scandal, highlight the importance of robust governance frameworks to prevent fraud and mismanagement.
4. Directors must regularly review and update governance practices, fostering a culture of openness, risk management, and stakeholder engagement.
5. Effective governance is not only about adhering to legal and regulatory requirements but also about maintaining ethical standards and making decisions in the best interests of all stakeholders.

Good corporate governance is the backbone of a successful organisation, promoting sustainable growth, building investor confidence, and minimising risk.

Chapter 12

Code of Conduct

A Code of Conduct serves as the ethical backbone of any organisation. It establishes the standards of behaviour expected from everyone—from the boardroom to the front line—ensuring alignment with the company's values, legal obligations, and social responsibilities. For directors, the Code of Conduct is more than a set of guidelines; it is a cornerstone of integrity, trust, and accountability in corporate governance.

Implementing a Code of Conduct is essential for fostering an ethical culture within an organisation. It addresses critical issues such as conflicts of interest, transparency, fair treatment of employees, and the ethical management of relationships with external stakeholders. By serving as a safeguard against unethical practices, it enhances the company's reputation and builds long-term value for shareholders. This chapter delves into the significance of a Code of Conduct, the steps to develop one, and its pivotal role in corporate governance.

Example: PepsiCo's Commitment to Ethical Business Practices

A compelling example of a Code of Conduct in action can be found in PepsiCo. The company's Code of Conduct, known as the "PepsiCo Global Code of Conduct," emphasises its commitment to ethical behaviour, transparency, and compliance with laws and regulations. It is designed to guide employees and directors in making decisions aligned with PepsiCo's core values: respect, integrity, accountability, and collaboration.

This ethical framework was put to the test during the 2010 palm oil supply chain controversy. Advocacy groups accused the company of sourcing palm oil linked to deforestation and unethical labour practices. Recognising the potential damage to its reputation and values, PepsiCo's leadership relied on their Code of Conduct to address the situation.

The company took decisive action, launching an independent investigation into its supply chain practices and committing to sourcing 100% sustainable palm oil. They engaged with NGOs, suppliers, and industry stakeholders to develop a robust, transparent supply chain strategy. By holding itself accountable to its ethical standards, PepsiCo not only resolved the immediate issue but also strengthened its commitment to sustainability and human rights, earning back the trust of stakeholders and customers.

This example underscores how a well-crafted and enforced Code of Conduct can act as a guide through complex challenges. It helps organisations navigate ethical dilemmas with integrity and demonstrates the importance of aligning business decisions with the company's values and principles.

Practical Tips for Directors on Establishing a Code of Conduct

1. **Defining the Company's Core Values**

    The first step in developing a Code of Conduct is identifying the company's core values. These values will form the foundation of the code and guide decisions. Directors should ask:

    - What principles define how we do business?
    - What ethical standards do we uphold in our relationships with customers, employees, and the community?

Common principles include:

- Integrity and honesty
- Transparency and accountability
- Respect for diversity and inclusion
- Responsibility towards the environment
- Commitment to fairness and equality

2. Clear and Comprehensive Guidelines

Once the core values are defined, the next step is to create clear guidelines that provide specific instructions for how employees should behave in various situations. The guidelines should address common issues such as:

- **Conflicts of Interest:** Directors and employees must avoid situations where personal interests conflict with the company's interests.
- **Confidentiality and Data Protection:** Protecting sensitive company and client information is paramount.
- **Compliance with Laws:** Adherence to local and international laws, including anti-corruption and anti-money laundering regulations.
- **Diversity and Equal Opportunity:** The Code should support non-discriminatory practices and encourage diversity.

3. Training and Awareness

Implementing the Code of Conduct is only effective if all employees and directors are well-informed and regularly reminded of its content. Directors should:

- Establish **training programmes** for new hires and regular refreshers for existing employees.
- Promote **open communication channels** where employees feel comfortable discussing concerns and asking questions about ethical dilemmas.

4. Enforcing the Code

A Code of Conduct is only valuable if it is actively enforced. Directors should:

- Establish **mechanisms for reporting violations**, such as a whistleblower hotline, ensuring that employees feel safe reporting unethical behaviour.
- Ensure that there are clear **consequences for breaches** of the Code, which should be enforced consistently and fairly.

5. Regular Reviews and Updates

A Code of Conduct should not be static. It must evolve to reflect changes in the organisation, the legal landscape, and societal expectations. Directors should:

- **Regularly review** the code to ensure it remains relevant.
- **Update** it as needed to reflect new laws or ethical concerns, such as emerging issues in data privacy or sustainability practices.

Table: Companies with Strong Ethical Standards

Company	Ethical Focus	Outcome
Johnson & Johnson	Strong commitment to public safety and health	Resilience during crises, maintaining trust
Patagonia	Environmental responsibility and transparency	Increased customer loyalty and brand strength
Unilever	Commitment to sustainability and social responsibility	Long-term growth and shareholder value

Interactive Element: Code of Conduct Implementation Checklist

Evaluate your company's Code of Conduct using this checklist:

1. Are the company's core values clearly defined and aligned with ethical standards?
2. Does the code provide clear guidance on key areas such as conflicts of interest and confidentiality?
3. Is there an accessible and effective training programme for all employees?
4. Does the code have mechanisms in place for reporting unethical behaviour?
5. Is there a process for reviewing and updating the code regularly?
6. Are violations of the code met with consistent and appropriate consequences?

Discussion Question:

How can directors effectively balance the enforcement of the Code of Conduct with the need for flexibility in decision-making, especially in complex or competitive environments?

Key Takeaways

1. **A Code of Conduct is Essential:** It provides a framework for ethical decision-making and behaviour across all levels of the organisation.
2. **Values Drive Actions:** The core values of the company should guide the development of the Code and influence all decisions.
3. **Training and Enforcement are Critical:** A Code is only effective when it is regularly communicated, consistently enforced, and backed by a culture of integrity.
4. **Regular Updates Ensure Relevance:** A Code of Conduct should evolve to address new challenges, such as technological advances or changes in regulatory frameworks.
5. **Long-Term Benefits:** Companies with strong ethical standards, like Johnson & Johnson, enjoy greater trust, resilience in crises, and sustained business success.

A well-crafted and thoughtfully implemented Code of Conduct not only helps protect a company's reputation but also fosters a culture of accountability and transparency. Directors who champion ethical leadership will lead organisations that thrive in the long term, driven by the confidence of all stakeholders.

Chapter 13

Risk Management

Understanding the Importance of Risk Management

Risk management is the process of identifying, assessing, and managing potential risks that could threaten the viability of an organisation. In the context of corporate governance, risk management is not just about protecting assets but also about ensuring the long-term sustainability and growth of a business. A robust risk management framework is crucial for boards of directors because it allows them to anticipate and mitigate risks that could negatively impact the company's strategy, operations, or reputation.

For directors, having a comprehensive understanding of risk management is essential, as they are ultimately responsible for overseeing the identification and management of risks within the organisation. Effective risk management helps boards make informed decisions, protect the company's assets, and ensure compliance with legal and regulatory requirements. It also provides a competitive advantage by enabling organisations to take calculated risks and pursue opportunities with confidence.

Risk management is not a one-time exercise but an ongoing, dynamic process that evolves with the business environment. As markets and industries change, new risks emerge, requiring boards to remain vigilant and adaptable. Directors must ensure that risk management practices are integrated into the company's strategy, governance, and operations to safeguard the organisation against potential crises.

Example: The Case of Johnson & Johnson's Tylenol Crisis

A historical example of effective risk management is Johnson & Johnson's handling of the Tylenol cyanide crisis in 1982. In this case, seven people died in the Chicago area after ingesting Tylenol capsules that had been tampered with and laced with cyanide. Despite the catastrophic nature of the event, Johnson & Johnson's quick and decisive response is considered a textbook example of crisis management.

What made Johnson & Johnson's response effective?

1. **Proactive Risk Identification**: The company immediately recognised the potential for harm and took swift action to contain the issue. They did not wait for further incidents to occur before acting.
2. **Clear and Transparent Communication**: The company communicated openly with the public, regulators, and customers, ensuring transparency and maintaining trust throughout the crisis.
3. **Stakeholder Engagement**: Johnson & Johnson prioritised customer safety above profits, recalling 31 million bottles of Tylenol and implementing tamper-evident packaging, which set new industry standards.
4. **Strategic Recovery Plan**: The company's swift actions allowed them to regain market share within a year, despite the negative impact on their brand.

This case highlights the importance of having a crisis management plan and risk management framework in place to deal with unexpected threats. Johnson & Johnson's successful recovery demonstrates how proactive risk management and a well-executed response can turn a potential disaster into an opportunity for rebuilding brand loyalty and trust.

Identifying, Assessing, and Mitigating Risks

Risk management is a multi-step process that involves identifying, assessing, and mitigating risks. Each step is critical to ensuring that the board and management understand the full scope of potential threats to the business and are equipped to handle them effectively.

1. Risk Identification

The first step in risk management is identifying the potential risks that could affect the organisation. This process involves examining internal and external factors that could negatively impact the company's objectives. Common categories of risks include:

- **Strategic Risks**: Risks that arise from changes in the competitive landscape, shifts in market demand, or changes in regulatory policies.
- **Operational Risks**: Risks associated with the day-to-day operations of the business, including supply chain disruptions, technology failures, or human resource challenges.
- **Financial Risks**: Risks related to financial performance, such as cash flow issues, currency fluctuations, or exposure to interest rate changes.
- **Reputational Risks**: Risks that could harm the company's brand, customer loyalty, or public image, often arising from negative media coverage, scandals, or customer dissatisfaction.
- **Compliance and Legal Risks**: Risks related to non-compliance with laws, regulations, or industry standards that could lead to legal penalties, fines, or litigation.

Boards should ensure that risk identification is a collaborative process, involving all levels of the organisation. Risk identification should also be dynamic, continuously monitored, and updated to reflect newly emerging risks.

2. Risk Assessment

Once risks are identified, the next step is assessing their potential impact and likelihood. Risk assessment involves evaluating each identified risk on two key factors:

- **Impact:** The severity of the potential consequences if the risk were to materialise. This can be financial, reputational, or operational in nature.
- **Likelihood:** The probability that the risk will occur. This is often based on historical data, industry trends, or expert opinions.

Risk assessment helps prioritise risks based on their potential impact and likelihood, allowing the board to allocate resources efficiently. Tools such as risk matrices and heat maps are often used to visualise and evaluate risks based on these criteria.

3. Risk Mitigation

After assessing the risks, boards must develop strategies to mitigate or manage those risks. Risk mitigation involves implementing measures that reduce the likelihood of a risk occurring or minimising its impact if it does occur. Common risk mitigation strategies include:

- **Risk Avoidance:** Changing business practices or strategies to eliminate the risk entirely. For example, a company may decide not to enter a high-risk market.
- **Risk Reduction:** Implementing controls to reduce the probability or severity of a risk. This could include strengthening cybersecurity measures to mitigate the risk of a data breach.
- **Risk Transfer:** Shifting the risk to another party, such as purchasing insurance or outsourcing high-risk operations to a third party.
- **Risk Acceptance:** In some cases, a company may decide to accept the risk, particularly if the potential reward outweighs the risk, or if the likelihood of occurrence is minimal.

A risk management strategy should involve a combination of these approaches, depending on the nature of the risk and the company's resources.

Practical Tips for Directors on Risk Management

1. **Integrate Risk Management into the Company Culture**

   Risk management should not be a standalone activity but an integral part of the company's culture. Directors should promote a risk-aware culture across the organisation, ensuring that employees at all levels understand the importance of identifying and reporting risks.

   - *Tip*: Establish regular risk management training for employees and senior leaders to ensure that everyone understands their role in managing risk.

2. **Establish a Risk Management Committee**

   While the board of directors is ultimately responsible for overseeing risk management, establishing a dedicated risk management committee can help provide focus and expertise in this area. This committee can be tasked with identifying emerging risks, reviewing risk assessments, and recommending mitigation strategies.

- *Tip*: Ensure that the risk management committee includes individuals with diverse skill sets and backgrounds, such as finance, operations, and legal expertise, to bring a comprehensive perspective on risk.

3. **Monitor and Review Risk Continuously**

Risk management is an ongoing process. Risks evolve, new risks emerge, and existing risks may change in severity. Directors should ensure that risk management practices are regularly reviewed and updated to reflect changes in the business environment.

- *Tip*: Conduct quarterly or annual reviews of the company's risk management framework and adjust strategies as necessary.

4. **Implement Scenario Planning**

Scenario planning helps boards prepare for potential risks by modelling different scenarios and assessing how the company would respond. This can be particularly useful for strategic risks or crises that are difficult to predict but could have a significant impact.

- *Tip*: Regularly engage in scenario planning exercises to help identify potential risks and ensure that the company is prepared for the unexpected.

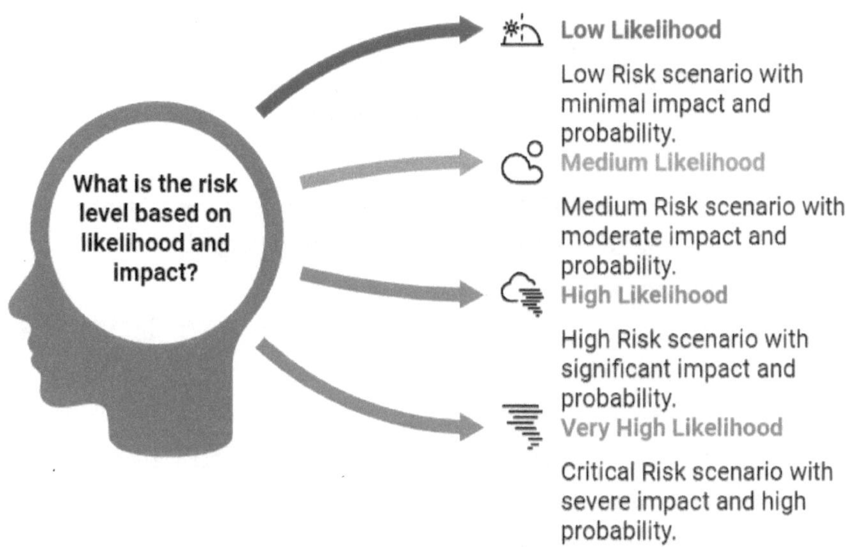

Low Risk scenario with minimal impact and probability.

Medium Risk scenario with moderate impact and probability.

High Risk scenario with significant impact and probability.

Critical Risk scenario with severe impact and high probability.

Interactive Element: Risk Management Checklist

Evaluate your company's risk management framework using the following checklist:

1. Has your board identified and categorised all significant risks to the organisation?
2. Is the risk management process integrated into the company's overall strategy?
3. Do you have a dedicated risk management committee that reports to the board?
4. Are risks regularly assessed and monitored for potential changes?
5. Are risk mitigation strategies documented and regularly reviewed for effectiveness?
6. Do employees at all levels understand the importance of identifying and reporting risks?

Key Takeaways

1. Risk management is an essential component of corporate governance, allowing boards to safeguard the organisation against potential threats.

2. The process of identifying, assessing, and mitigating risks ensures that the board is prepared for the unexpected and can make informed decisions.

3. Companies that integrate risk management into their culture and decision-making processes are better equipped to handle crises and capitalise on opportunities.

4. Proactive risk management, including scenario planning and continuous monitoring, can prevent or minimise the impact of risks on the organisation.

5. Directors should establish a dedicated risk management committee and ensure regular reviews of the company's risk management framework to keep pace with emerging risks.

By embedding a strong risk management culture and process within an organisation, boards can ensure resilience in the face of adversity, drive long-term value, and maintain stakeholder trust.

Chapter 14

Financial Reporting and Controls

In any organisation, financial integrity forms the foundation of trust, credibility, and long-term sustainability. For boards of directors, the responsibility to ensure accurate financial reporting and robust internal controls is paramount. In today's business environment, where stakeholders increasingly demand transparency and accountability, the board's role in overseeing financial accuracy is more critical than ever. It is not only about compliance with regulations but also about safeguarding the organisation's reputation, protecting shareholder interests, and facilitating sound decision-making.

Financial reporting serves as the cornerstone of investor relations, and the strength of internal controls can significantly influence a company's governance and risk management framework. The board must ensure that financial statements reflect a true and fair view of the company's financial position and performance while proactively mitigating financial risks such as fraud, errors, and misrepresentation.

This chapter examines the board's pivotal role in financial reporting and controls, explores key best practices, and offers actionable guidance for directors. We will also discuss a recent case of financial mismanagement to highlight the consequences of oversight failure and the importance of a strong control environment.

Example: The Wirecard Scandal and the Failure of Oversight

The collapse of Wirecard AG, a German fintech giant, serves as a stark reminder of the importance of financial oversight. Wirecard was once heralded as a symbol of Europe's technological advancement, with a market valuation exceeding €24 billion at its peak. However, in 2020, it was revealed that €1.9 billion—reported as held in escrow accounts—simply did not exist.

The scandal exposed deep weaknesses in Wirecard's governance, with its board failing to exercise adequate oversight over financial reporting and internal controls. Despite red flags raised by whistleblowers, investigative journalists, and short sellers over several years, Wirecard's board largely dismissed these concerns. The company's external auditors also failed to detect the fraud, signing off on financial statements that grossly misrepresented its financial health.

Wirecard's fraudulent practices included fictitious transactions, inflated revenues, and misallocated funds, all concealed through opaque corporate structures and complicity from certain executives. When the truth emerged, the company filed for insolvency, leaving investors, creditors, and employees to face massive losses.

The failure of Wirecard's board highlights several critical lessons for directors:

- **Proactive Oversight**: The board must challenge management assumptions and ensure that financial reporting is accurate and verifiable. Passive acceptance of information can lead to disastrous outcomes.
- **Whistleblower Support**: Encouraging and protecting whistleblowers is vital. In Wirecard's case, dismissing credible warnings allowed the fraud to persist for years.
- **Independent Audits**: Boards must demand accountability from external auditors and, when necessary, seek independent reviews of financial statements.
- **Robust Internal Controls**: Wirecard lacked effective internal controls to monitor its global operations, enabling executives to manipulate financial data with ease.

Practical Tips for Directors on Financial Reporting and Controls

1. Understand the Key Financial Statements

For effective oversight, directors must have a solid understanding of the company's key financial statements:

- **Income Statement:** Shows the company's profitability over a specific period.
- **Balance Sheet:** Provides a snapshot of the company's assets, liabilities, and equity at a specific point in time.
- **Cash Flow Statement:** Highlights the company's cash inflows and outflows, critical for assessing liquidity and operational efficiency.

Directors should ensure that these statements are not only accurate but also reflect the true financial health of the company. They should work closely with the finance team to understand the key assumptions and estimates behind the figures presented.

2. Promote Transparency and Clarity

A key responsibility of the board is to ensure that financial reports are transparent, accurate, and easily understandable for all stakeholders, including investors, regulators, and employees. Directors should:

- Encourage clear and concise financial disclosures, including the breakdown of complex financial instruments and transactions.
- Ensure that management is forthcoming about financial risks, uncertainties, and assumptions.

For example, if the company uses complex financial products such as derivatives or engages in cross-border transactions, these should be disclosed in a straightforward manner to avoid misleading stakeholders.

3. Establish Robust Internal Controls

Internal controls are the policies and procedures put in place to safeguard company assets, ensure financial accuracy, and prevent fraud. The board should:

- Oversee the design and implementation of a strong internal control framework.
- Ensure that the internal audit function is independent and effective, reporting directly to the audit committee.
- Regularly review and test the controls to ensure they are functioning as intended.

The board should also ensure that there is a segregation of duties to prevent any individual from having too much control over financial processes, thereby reducing the risk of fraud or errors.

4. Evaluate the Role of the External Auditor

External auditors play a key role in ensuring the accuracy of financial reports. The board's audit committee should:

- Review the selection of the external auditor and ensure that they are independent.
- Discuss the scope of the audit with the external auditor to ensure that all relevant areas are covered.
- Evaluate the effectiveness of the external audit and review their findings to ensure that any issues are addressed promptly.

Directors should not take the auditor's opinion at face value but should question any areas of concern raised during the audit.

5. Monitor and Address Financial Risks

Directors must remain vigilant about potential financial risks, both internal and external. These risks may include liquidity issues, foreign exchange fluctuations, cybersecurity threats, or regulatory changes. The board should:

- Regularly review risk management reports and ensure that financial risks are adequately mitigated.
- Ensure that management has the tools and processes in place to monitor and report on risks effectively.

A proactive approach to risk management can prevent many financial missteps and help the company navigate complex environments.

Table: Key Financial Oversight Metrics

Metric	Description	Importance for the Board
Audit Independence	The independence of the external auditor	Ensures the auditor's objectivity in reviewing financial statements
Internal Control Strength	The effectiveness of internal controls	Prevents fraud and ensures accurate financial reporting
Financial Risk Exposure	The company's exposure to financial risks	Helps the board understand the risk landscape and make informed decisions
Audit Committee Reporting	The frequency and detail of audit committee reports	Provides insights into financial reporting oversight and potential issues

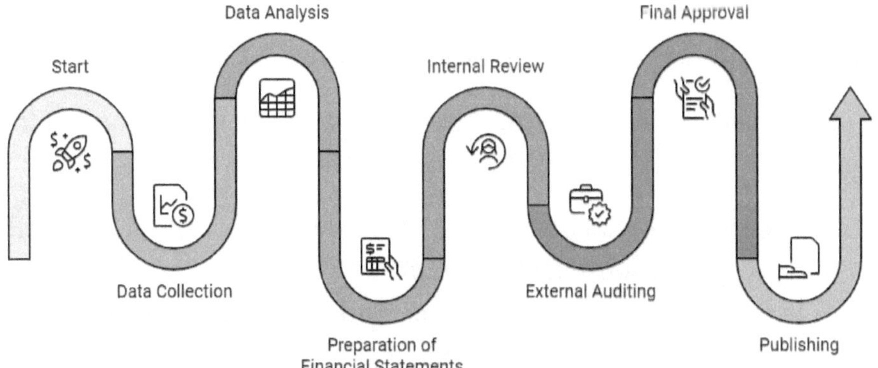

Interactive Element: Financial Oversight Checklist

Directors can use the following checklist to evaluate the strength of the company's financial reporting and internal controls:

1. **Are the financial statements accurate and in compliance with relevant accounting standards?**
2. **Is there a clear line of communication between the board, the audit committee, and external auditors?**

3. **Are key financial assumptions disclosed transparently?**
4. **Does the company have a robust internal control framework in place?**
5. **Are financial risks being actively monitored and mitigated?**
6. **Is the external auditor independent and conducting thorough reviews of financial statements?**
7. **Are there regular reviews of internal financial reporting processes and controls?**

Discussion Question:

How can the board balance the need for thorough financial oversight with the understanding that financial performance can fluctuate due to market conditions or strategic decisions? Should there be limits on the depth of intervention in day-to-day financial management?

Key Takeaways

1. **Financial Reporting Integrity is Essential:** The board must ensure that financial statements are accurate and provide a true reflection of the company's financial health.
2. **Robust Internal Controls Are Critical:** Strong internal controls protect against fraud and ensure the accuracy of financial reporting.
3. **Transparency Drives Trust:** Clear, transparent financial reporting builds trust with investors and other stakeholders, reinforcing corporate governance.
4. **Continuous Monitoring is Necessary:** Regular reviews of financial reporting, controls, and risk management processes ensure that potential issues are addressed before they become crises.
5. **Financial Oversight Should Be Proactive, Not Reactive:** Directors must actively monitor financial processes and address potential risks before they impact the company's performance.

By prioritising strong financial reporting and controls, the board not only helps protect the organisation from financial scandals but also enhances the long-term value and sustainability of the company. Through diligent oversight, directors can ensure that the company operates with transparency, integrity, and accountability, benefiting all stakeholders.

Chapter 15

Internal Audit

Internal audit is a key component of a strong corporate governance framework, providing an independent and objective assessment of a company's financial and operational activities. The primary function of internal audit is to evaluate and improve the effectiveness of risk management, control, and governance processes. For directors, understanding the role and importance of internal audit is critical in ensuring that an organisation adheres to the highest standards of accountability, integrity, and compliance.

The internal audit function serves as a crucial line of defence against fraud, errors, inefficiencies, and regulatory violations. It helps the board of directors maintain confidence that the organisation is operating effectively, resources are being used efficiently, and risks are being appropriately managed. In addition, it plays an essential role in ensuring that financial reporting is accurate and that internal controls are functioning as intended.

In this chapter, we will explore the importance of internal audit within governance, share real-world examples of its impact, provide practical guidance for directors on overseeing the internal audit function, and highlight best practices to ensure its effectiveness. By doing so, we aim to underscore the value of internal audit as a strategic tool for organisational success and risk mitigation.

Example: The Role of Internal Audit in Preventing the WorldCom Scandal

In the early 2000s, **WorldCom**, once one of the largest telecommunications companies in the United States, became embroiled in one of the largest corporate accounting scandals in history. The company's management had engaged in massive fraudulent accounting practices, including the misstatement of expenses and the inflation of assets to the tune of over $11 billion. The fraud, which was not detected by external auditors, was eventually uncovered by an internal auditor named **Cynthia Cooper.**

Cooper, who worked for WorldCom's internal audit department, noticed irregularities in the company's financial statements, particularly concerning the capitalisation of ordinary operating expenses. Despite the company's pressure to ignore the discrepancies, Cooper persisted in her investigation. Her diligence in reporting the issues to the board ultimately led to the exposure of the fraud, saving the company from further financial and reputational damage.

The case of WorldCom illustrates the critical importance of internal audit in detecting and preventing fraud. Although external audits are essential, it was the internal audit function that played a pivotal role in uncovering the fraudulent activities. It highlights how a well-established internal audit function, empowered with the independence and authority to report directly to the board, can act as an early warning system for issues that could otherwise undermine the organisation's integrity.

Practical Tips for Directors on Overseeing Internal Audit

1. **Ensure Independence and Objectivity**

    For internal audit to function effectively, it must be independent of management. Directors should ensure that the internal audit department has direct access to the audit committee or the board of directors, rather than reporting solely to the CEO or CFO. This independence enables auditors to provide unbiased assessments of the organisation's operations, without fear of retaliation or influence from management.

- **Best Practice:** Establish a formal reporting structure where the head of internal audit reports directly to the audit committee or the board.

2. **Clearly Define the Scope and Responsibilities**

Directors should work with the internal audit function to clearly define its role, scope, and objectives. Internal auditors should focus on areas that are most critical to the organisation's success, including financial reporting, regulatory compliance, risk management, and operational efficiency. The scope should be regularly reviewed and updated to address emerging risks and issues.

- **Best Practice:** Conduct annual risk assessments in collaboration with the internal audit team to ensure that the audit plan aligns with the company's current risk profile.

3. **Foster a Strong Relationship with Management**

While the internal audit function must remain independent, it should also maintain a collaborative relationship with management. Directors should encourage management to view internal audit as a valuable partner in improving processes, not just as an entity that finds fault. Effective communication between internal audit and management can help ensure that audit recommendations are implemented and that issues are addressed proactively.

- **Best Practice:** Organise regular meetings between internal audit and senior management to discuss audit findings, recommendations, and progress on corrective actions.

4. **Focus on Risk-Based Audits**

Internal audits should be risk-based, focusing on areas of highest concern to the company. This includes financial reporting risks, regulatory compliance, fraud risks, and cybersecurity threats.

The board should ensure that internal audit resources are allocated to areas that pose the greatest potential impact on the organisation's operations and reputation.

- **Best Practice:** Ensure that the internal audit function uses data analytics and other tools to assess areas of risk more effectively, especially when monitoring high-risk activities like financial reporting or fraud prevention.

5. **Review Audit Findings and Ensure Corrective Action**

The board must not only review internal audit findings but also ensure that management takes appropriate corrective action. Internal audit recommendations should be followed up with specific timelines for resolution, and progress should be monitored regularly. Directors must hold management accountable for addressing audit findings and resolving issues promptly.

- **Best Practice:** Use a formal tracking system to monitor the progress of corrective actions and report on them at board meetings.

6. **Continuous Improvement of Internal Audit**

The internal audit function itself should undergo continuous improvement. Directors should ensure that the audit team has access to the latest training, tools, and technologies to stay ahead of emerging risks. In addition, internal auditors should be encouraged to innovate and use their findings to improve organisational processes.

- **Best Practice:** Support internal audit participation in professional development programmes and consider implementing technology solutions to enhance the audit process, such as automated audit software and data analytics tools.

Table: Common Risks Addressed by Internal Audit

Risk Area	Description	Audit Focus
Financial Misstatement	Inaccuracies in financial reporting	Review financial statements and accounting practices
Fraud	Intentional misrepresentation of data	Conduct fraud risk assessments and control tests
Compliance Risk	Failure to comply with regulations	Review adherence to laws, regulations, and internal policies
Operational Efficiency	Waste of resources and inefficiencies	Evaluate business processes for optimization opportunities
Cybersecurity Risk	Data breaches and IT security threats	Assess cybersecurity protocols and data protection measures

Governance and Audit Structure

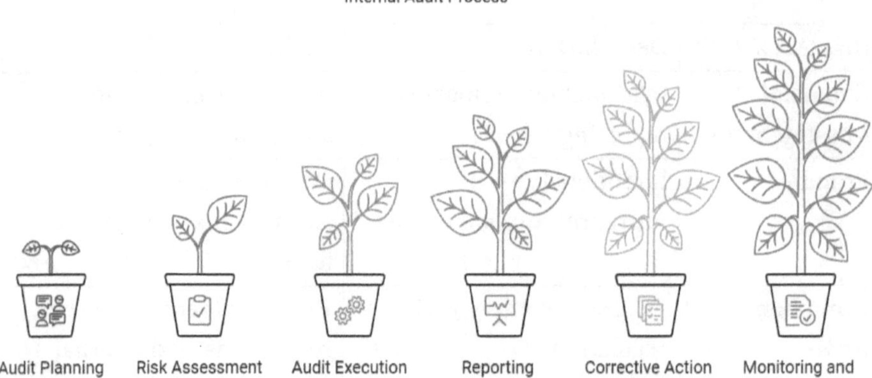

Interactive Element: Internal Audit Effectiveness Checklist

Directors can use the following checklist to evaluate the effectiveness of their internal audit function:

1. **Is the internal audit function independent from management?**

   - Yes / No

2. **Does the internal audit function have direct access to the board or audit committee?**

   - Yes / No

3. **Are the internal audit scope and objectives aligned with the company's risk profile?**

   - Yes / No

4. **Is internal audit work focused on the highest-risk areas?**

   - Yes / No

5. **Does the internal audit function receive adequate resources, training, and tools to perform its duties?**

   - Yes / No

6. **Are management and the board committed to implementing corrective actions based on internal audit findings?**

   - Yes / No

7. **Is there a system in place to track and report on the progress of audit recommendations?**

   - Yes / No

Discussion Question:

How can the internal audit function balance its role as an independent evaluator while fostering a cooperative relationship with management to drive improvements within the organisation?

Key Takeaways

1. **Internal Audit is Essential for Risk Management:** The internal audit function provides independent assurance that the company's risk management, control, and governance processes are functioning effectively.
2. **Independence is Critical:** For internal audit to be effective, it must maintain independence from management, reporting directly to the audit committee or board.
3. **Focus on High-Risk Areas:** Directors should ensure that internal audit focuses on the company's highest risks, including financial misstatements, fraud, and regulatory compliance.
4. **Collaboration Enhances Effectiveness:** A collaborative relationship between internal audit and management ensures that audit findings lead to meaningful changes and improvements.
5. **Continuous Improvement is Key:** The internal audit function should be continually enhanced through training, technology, and process improvements to keep up with emerging risks.

By prioritising the independence, effectiveness, and resource allocation of the internal audit function, directors can help ensure that their organisation remains compliant, efficient, and resilient to financial and operational risks. Internal audit plays a vital role in maintaining the integrity and sustainability of an organisation, safeguarding the company's long-term success.

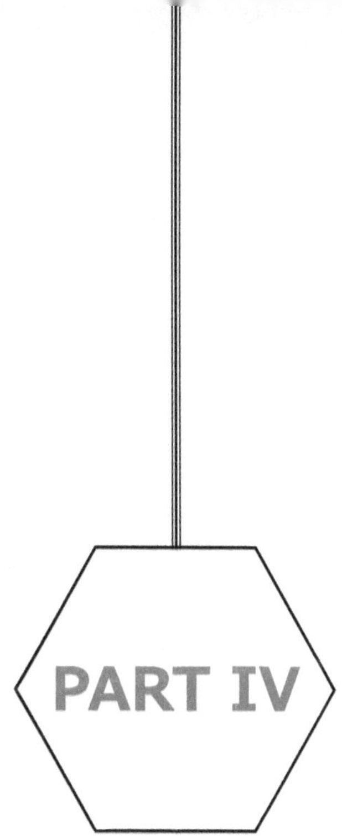

The Board's Role in Strategic Planning

Chapter 16

The Board's Role in Strategic Planning

Understanding the Board's Role in Strategic Planning

Strategic planning is a cornerstone of corporate governance, representing a company's roadmap for the future. While management is responsible for implementing the strategy, the board of directors has the critical role of guiding, overseeing, and ensuring that the strategy aligns with the company's long-term objectives and the interests of shareholders. In this chapter, we will explore the board's essential function in the strategic planning process, its contribution to setting direction, overseeing execution, and adapting strategies to meet evolving challenges in the business environment.

Effective strategic planning requires directors to take an active, yet impartial, approach—ensuring that the strategy is not only visionary but also grounded in practicality and sustainability. Board members should ask the right questions, challenge assumptions, and ensure that the strategy reflects both current realities and future possibilities. This involvement is essential because poor strategic decisions can lead to missed opportunities, and ill-preparedness for external challenges can jeopardise a company's long-term viability.

The board's role in strategic planning is multifaceted. Directors provide oversight, contribute insights from their experience, and ensure that management is executing the strategy effectively. However, the board's role is not passive. It actively drives discussions about strategy, evaluates risks, and ensures that the company's long-term goals align with its overall mission and values. With this level of involvement, the board helps ensure that the organisation stays on course and remains adaptable in an ever-changing business landscape.

Example: The Strategic Turnaround of Starbucks under Howard Schultz

A powerful example of the board's role in strategic planning is the turnaround story of Starbucks during the late 2000s under the leadership of Howard Schultz. By 2008, Starbucks was grappling with declining sales, over-expansion, and a loss of its unique customer experience. Schultz, who had previously stepped down as CEO, returned to the helm with a bold vision to revitalise the brand and restore its focus on quality and customer connection.

One of Schultz's first actions was to temporarily close over 7,000 stores to retrain baristas, signalling a commitment to quality. The board played a critical role in supporting this high-stakes decision, understanding the potential short-term financial impact while appreciating the long-term strategic benefits. Schultz and his leadership team worked closely with the board, presenting clear and focused plans that prioritised enhancing the in-store experience, streamlining operations, and leveraging digital innovation.

For example, the introduction of Starbucks Rewards and mobile payment systems was a significant pivot towards embracing technology to deepen customer loyalty. The board's alignment with Schultz's vision ensured that resources were allocated effectively and that the company stayed focused on its core values and strengths.

This strategic pivot, supported by engaged board oversight, transformed Starbucks from a struggling brand into a global leader in the coffee industry. The case of Starbucks highlights the importance of a board that trusts leadership while actively engaging in strategic discussions, fostering the alignment needed to drive transformative change.

Practical Tips for Directors: How to Contribute to Strategic Planning

Directors play an integral role in the development and oversight of the company's strategy. To effectively contribute to strategic planning, directors can consider the following best practices:

1. **Engage Early and Often:** Boards should begin their involvement in strategic planning well in advance of formal meetings. By meeting early in the process and being engaged throughout, directors can ensure they have a deep understanding of the strategy before it is presented for final approval. Regular check-ins with management throughout the year also allow boards to stay informed and provide valuable input.

2. **Understand Market Trends and External Forces:** Directors must stay abreast of market trends, competitive pressures, technological advancements, and regulatory changes. These external forces often shape the strategic direction and present both risks and opportunities. By having a comprehensive understanding of the external environment, directors can ensure that the strategy is responsive and adaptable.

3. **Provide Objective Feedback and Challenge Assumptions:** One of the most valuable contributions a board can make is to provide critical feedback. Directors should question assumptions, challenge ideas that appear overly optimistic, and ensure that management has considered potential risks. Healthy debate and a willingness to challenge the status quo can strengthen the overall strategy.

4. **Ensure Alignment with Company Values:** A successful strategy should reflect the company's values, mission, and vision. Directors must ensure that the strategy doesn't deviate from these core principles, as a misalignment between strategy and company values can lead to long-term damage to the brand and reputation.

5. **Foster a Culture of Accountability:** The board must help set expectations for performance and hold management accountable for executing the strategy. Clear milestones and KPIs (Key Performance Indicators) should be established so that the progress of the strategy can be monitored. Regular updates on performance and corrective actions, if necessary, will keep the company on track.

6. **Balance Risk and Innovation:** Directors should assess the level of risk involved in a strategic plan and ensure that there is a balance between pursuing innovative opportunities and safeguarding the company's long-term financial health. This involves actively engaging in risk management discussions and ensuring that the company has sufficient risk mitigation plans in place.

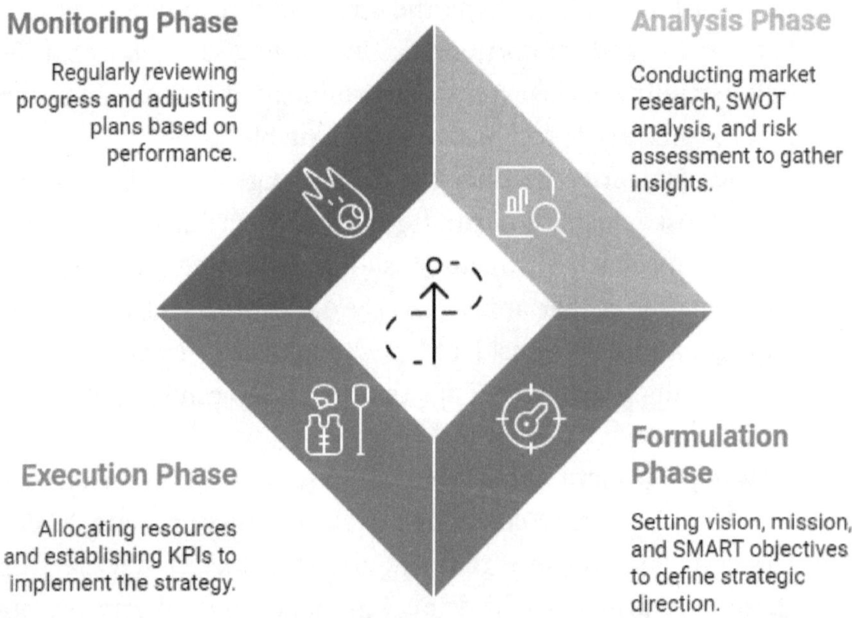

Interactive Element: Strategic Planning Discussion Questions

To engage directors further, it is essential to ask thought-provoking questions that will help them evaluate their approach to strategic planning. Here are a few discussion questions for board members to consider:

1. **What are the current strengths and weaknesses of our strategic plan?**
2. **Are we being overly cautious, or are we taking enough calculated risks in our strategy?**
3. **How does our strategy differentiate us from our competitors?**
4. **Are we considering long-term trends that may disrupt our industry, and how are we preparing for them?**
5. **How do we ensure alignment between the company's day-to-day operations and its long-term strategic objectives?**
6. **What role should the board play in adjusting the strategy if performance is not meeting expectations?**

These questions can be used as a guide for board discussions during strategic planning meetings, helping ensure that all aspects of the strategy are thoroughly considered.

Key Takeaways & Summary

1. The board's involvement in strategic planning is crucial for ensuring that the company's long-term vision is both ambitious and achievable.
2. Directors must engage early, understand market trends, challenge assumptions, and ensure that the strategy aligns with the company's core values.
3. Successful strategic planning involves collaboration between the board and management, with clear goals, regular monitoring, and adjustments as needed.

4. A case study of Apple highlights how a successful strategic pivot, supported by an engaged board, can transform a company's future.

5. Directors should foster a culture of accountability and balance risk and innovation in the strategic process.

Strategic planning is an ongoing, dynamic process that requires active and informed participation from the board. By providing leadership, oversight, and challenge, directors ensure that the company remains on track to achieve its long-term objectives and stay resilient in a competitive environment.

Chapter 17

Performance Management

Effective performance management is a cornerstone of strong corporate governance. For boards of directors, setting clear and measurable key performance indicators (KPIs) and consistently monitoring performance are critical to ensuring that the organisation is on track to meet its strategic goals and objectives. Performance management involves not just assessing the company's financial outcomes but also measuring the efficiency and effectiveness of operations, employee productivity, innovation, and overall organisational health.

The board's role in performance management is to provide oversight and strategic guidance, ensuring that performance is aligned with long-term objectives, shareholder expectations, and stakeholder interests. This function is vital for sustaining growth, identifying areas of improvement, and making informed decisions. Directors must foster a culture where performance is regularly assessed, feedback is constructive, and accountability is encouraged at all levels of the organisation.

In this chapter, we will explore how boards set KPIs, track performance, and respond to deviations from expected results. We will highlight both successful and failed performance management examples, providing practical insights and actionable advice to guide directors in establishing effective performance management systems for their organisations.

Example: Nokia's Decline – A Lesson in Performance Management

One of the most notable examples of failed performance management is **Nokia**, once the global leader in mobile phones. Throughout the early 2000s, Nokia dominated the market with its innovative products, capturing nearly 40% of the global mobile phone market share. However, by the late 2000s, Nokia began to lose its competitive edge. Despite market shifts, technological advancements, and increasing competition from the likes of Apple and Android, Nokia continued to rely on outdated business models and failed to adapt quickly enough.

Nokia's board struggled with effectively managing and monitoring performance in a rapidly changing industry. Key performance indicators (KPIs) like market share, profit margins, and brand loyalty, which had once been strong indicators of success, failed to capture the looming challenges the company faced. The leadership failed to take proactive steps to innovate and adjust to the market dynamics—especially the shift towards smartphones with touch interfaces and app ecosystems.

As a result, by the time Nokia attempted to pivot by partnering with Microsoft and launching the Windows Phone platform, it was too late. The company's market share plummeted, and by 2014, Nokia's mobile division was sold to Microsoft, marking the end of an era.

The key lesson from Nokia's downfall is that while performance management systems can effectively track success indicators, failing to adapt KPIs to shifting industry trends and proactively managing change can lead to organisational decline. In this case, Nokia's inability to adjust its performance metrics to include innovation, customer experience, and emerging technologies contributed to its failure to foresee the risks of complacency.

Practical Tips for Directors on Setting and Monitoring KPIs

Setting and monitoring KPIs is vital for ensuring that the organisation is on track to achieve its strategic goals. Directors must oversee the development of KPIs that are aligned with the company's long-term vision, provide clarity to senior management, and foster accountability.

Here are some practical tips for directors to ensure effective performance management:

1. **Align KPIs with Strategic Goals**

   The first step in performance management is ensuring that the KPIs are aligned with the company's strategic objectives. Directors should work with management to ensure that the metrics used reflect the priorities of the business, whether that is growth, profitability, market share, or customer satisfaction.

   - **Best Practice:** Review and update KPIs annually to ensure they are in line with the company's evolving strategic goals. For example, if a company shifts its focus to sustainability, KPIs should include environmental impact metrics, waste reduction, or renewable energy usage.

2. **Make KPIs SMART**

   KPIs should be Specific, Measurable, Achievable, Relevant, and Time-bound (SMART). By ensuring that the KPIs meet these criteria, directors can ensure that the targets are clear, realistic, and actionable, helping the board and management focus on achieving measurable results.

   - **Best Practice:** For financial performance, set clear targets for revenue, profit margin, and return on investment. For operational performance, focus on metrics like process efficiency, customer satisfaction, or supply chain optimisation.

3. **Balance Short-Term and Long-Term KPIs**

   Directors should balance short-term operational performance with long-term strategic growth. Short-term KPIs may focus on financial results, market share, or efficiency, while long-term KPIs should align with growth, innovation, and organisational transformation.

- **Best Practice:** Incorporate a mix of both. Short-term KPIs may focus on quarterly earnings and operational efficiency, while long-term KPIs could include innovation, customer loyalty, brand equity, and market expansion.

4. **Focus on Leading and Lagging Indicators**

KPIs can be classified into leading and lagging indicators. Leading indicators predict future performance, while lagging indicators show results after an event has occurred. Directors should ensure that both types of indicators are part of the performance management system.

- **Best Practice:** Leading indicators could include customer acquisition rates or product development milestones, while lagging indicators could include revenue growth or profitability.

5. **Implement a Robust Monitoring System**

It's not enough to simply set KPIs; they must be regularly tracked and reviewed. Directors should ensure that the company has a robust system in place to monitor performance. This includes dashboards that provide real-time updates on critical KPIs and regular performance reviews to assess progress.

- **Best Practice:** Use software tools to automate KPI tracking and reporting. Tools like **Tableau** or **Power BI** can provide visual dashboards that help boards and management stay on top of performance metrics.

6. **Hold Management Accountable**

KPIs should be used not only to monitor performance but also to hold management accountable for delivering results. Directors must ensure that management is responsible for the KPIs they oversee and that consequences exist for underperformance.

- **Best Practice:** Establish performance-based compensation structures that tie executive bonuses to meeting or exceeding key performance targets.

7. **Regularly Review and Adapt KPIs**

The business landscape is constantly changing, and so should the KPIs. Directors should ensure that KPIs are reviewed regularly and adapted to reflect the company's strategic goals, market conditions, and emerging risks.

- **Best Practice:** Schedule quarterly reviews of KPIs with the board and management to ensure they remain relevant. If necessary, adjust the KPIs to address new challenges or opportunities.

Table: Common Performance Metrics for Different Business Functions

Business Function	Key Performance Indicator	Purpose
Finance	Return on Equity (ROE)	Measures profitability relative to shareholder equity
Sales	Sales Growth Rate	Tracks the growth of sales over a period
Customer Service	Customer Satisfaction (CSAT)	Measures customer contentment with services
Operations	Operational Efficiency (OEE)	Measures the efficiency of production processes
HR	Employee Turnover Rate	Tracks retention and employee satisfaction
Marketing	Brand Awareness and Engagement	Measures the reach and impact of marketing efforts

Interactive Element: Performance Management Evaluation Quiz

To help directors assess their approach to performance management, consider the following quiz:

1. **Are your KPIs aligned with the company's long-term strategic goals?**

    ○ Yes / No / Not Sure

2. **Do you use a balance of leading and lagging indicators to track performance?**

    ○ Yes / No / Not Sure

3. **Are your KPIs regularly reviewed and adjusted in response to changes in the business environment?**

    ○ Yes / No / Not Sure

4. **Does the board receive real-time updates on performance, or is reporting done retrospectively?**

    o   Real-time / Retrospective / Both

5. **Is there a clear process in place for holding management accountable for meeting KPIs?**

    o   Yes / No / Not Sure

6. **Are employees at all levels aware of the company's KPIs and how their performance contributes to them?**

    o   Yes / No / Not Sure

Discussion Question:

How can boards balance the need for accountability with the importance of fostering a culture of innovation when setting KPIs?

Key Takeaways

1. **KPIs are Integral to Governance:** KPIs serve as a guidepost for directors, enabling them to monitor performance, ensure alignment with strategic goals, and make informed decisions.
2. **SMART KPIs Drive Success:** KPIs must be specific, measurable, achievable, relevant, and time-bound to be effective in performance management.
3. **Balance Short-Term and Long-Term Goals:** Directors should set a balance between short-term performance measures and long-term strategic objectives to ensure sustainable success.
4. **Review and Adapt KPIs Regularly:** Performance management is a dynamic process. KPIs should be regularly assessed and adapted to reflect changes in the market, industry trends, and organisational priorities.

5. **Accountability is Key:** Holding management accountable for performance outcomes is essential for ensuring that KPIs are met and the organisation stays on track.

By adhering to these principles, boards can help guide their organisations towards long-term success, effectively managing performance while staying agile in response to changing business environments.

Chapter 18

Mergers and Acquisitions

The Board's Role in Mergers and Acquisitions (M&A)

Mergers and Acquisitions (M&A) are strategic corporate actions that can redefine the trajectory of a business. These transactions often result in significant shifts in the competitive landscape, with the potential for growth, diversification, or market consolidation. For boards of directors, the role in M&A decisions is paramount. They must assess, guide, and ultimately approve the acquisition or merger strategies, ensuring that these decisions align with the company's long-term objectives and the interests of shareholders.

M&A can bring numerous benefits, including market expansion, enhanced capabilities, cost efficiencies, and increased shareholder value. However, they also come with substantial risks—cultural integration challenges, regulatory hurdles, and financial complexities—that require careful oversight. This makes the board's involvement in the M&A process critical for success.

The board's role in M&A is multifaceted. It involves setting the strategic rationale for the transaction, overseeing the due diligence process, negotiating terms, and managing the post-deal integration. Boards also need to be acutely aware of the risks involved and ensure that all stakeholders, including employees, customers, and shareholders, are considered throughout the process.

This chapter will explore the board's responsibilities in M&A transactions, examine real-world examples of both successful and unsuccessful deals, provide practical guidance for directors involved in M&A, and outline actionable steps to ensure the deal adds value and aligns with the company's strategic vision.

Example: The Merger of Exxon and Mobil

One of the most successful M&A deals in corporate history was the merger of Exxon and Mobil in 1999, creating ExxonMobil, the world's largest publicly traded oil and gas company at the time. The deal, valued at approximately $81 billion, was considered a transformative step in the energy industry. The companies were already large players in the oil and gas sector, but by merging, they created an entity with enhanced economies of scale, a broader geographic footprint, and greater operational efficiencies.

The success of the ExxonMobil merger can be attributed to several key factors:

1. **Strategic Fit:** Both companies were in the same industry, with complementary strengths and market presences. The merger allowed them to combine their resources in exploration, refining, and distribution.

2. **Due Diligence:** The boards of both companies were heavily involved in the due diligence process, ensuring that the transaction was financially sound and legally compliant. Extensive analyses were performed on both companies' operations, assets, and liabilities.

3. **Clear Integration Plan:** ExxonMobil was able to successfully integrate the two companies' operations while maintaining a focus on cost reduction and operational efficiency. This strategic focus helped the combined company achieve significant savings and improve profitability.

4. **Strong Leadership:** The leadership team, led by former Exxon CEO Lee Raymond, played a pivotal role in steering the integration process. Raymond, alongside the ExxonMobil board,

ensured that the company's vision was clear, and that leadership was aligned with the strategic goals of the merger.

As a result, the merger became one of the most successful in corporate history, driving massive shareholder value and solidifying ExxonMobil's position as a global leader in the oil and gas industry.

Practical Guidance for Directors: Best Practices in M&A

Directors play an integral role in each phase of the M&A process, from initial strategic considerations to post-deal integration. To navigate the complexities of M&A, directors should keep the following best practices in mind:

1. **Set Clear Strategic Objectives:** Before pursuing any M&A deal, the board must first determine the strategic objectives. What are the goals of the transaction? Are they to enter a new market, acquire new technology, or achieve economies of scale? By understanding the strategic rationale, directors ensure that the transaction supports the company's long-term vision and enhances shareholder value.

2. **Conduct Rigorous Due Diligence:** Due diligence is critical in M&A transactions, and the board must ensure that it is thorough and unbiased. Directors should oversee the process of evaluating financial statements, assess potential risks, and identify legal or regulatory concerns. This step should also involve a detailed analysis of the target company's culture, operational capabilities, and human resources. A failure in due diligence can result in unexpected liabilities or integration challenges that may harm the company's reputation and financial standing.

3. **Establish Clear Governance and Roles:** One of the major risks in M&A is the lack of clear governance during the process.

Directors must ensure that roles and responsibilities are well defined between the board and senior management. The board should set the strategic vision while empowering management to execute the transaction, ensuring that there is no confusion or overlap of authority.

4. **Focus on Cultural Integration:** Cultural alignment is often a critical determinant in the success or failure of an M&A. Boards should assess not only the financials of a deal but also the cultural fit between the companies involved. Ensuring that leadership teams, values, and employee structures are aligned will reduce friction and increase the likelihood of a smooth integration process.

5. **Monitor Post-Deal Integration:** Post-merger integration can be just as challenging as the negotiation and acquisition phases. Directors should stay actively involved in overseeing integration efforts, ensuring that synergies are realised, and that operations are efficiently consolidated. It is crucial to track progress and address any issues that arise, especially in terms of organisational structure, employee retention, and customer relationships.

6. **Ensure Communication with Stakeholders:** Throughout the M&A process, communication with key stakeholders—employees, customers, and shareholders—is essential. Directors should ensure transparency and provide clear updates, as this helps maintain trust and reduces uncertainty. In particular, shareholders need to be informed of the strategic benefits of the deal and how it will impact the value of their investment.

M&A Process Overview

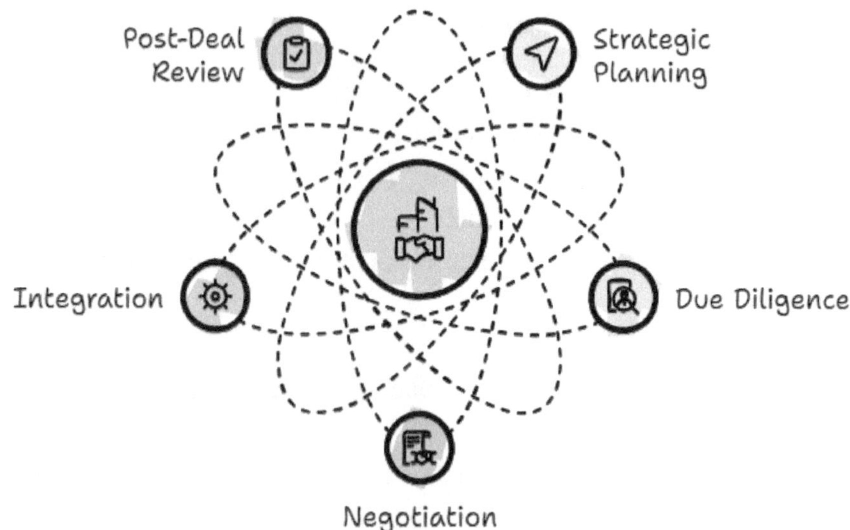

Interactive Element: M&A Checklist for Directors

Here is a checklist that directors can use to guide their participation in M&A transactions:

1. **Pre-Deal Strategy:**

   - Have we clearly defined the strategic rationale for this acquisition/merger?
   - Does the target company align with our long-term goals and values?
   - Are we considering the financial and cultural implications of the deal?

2. **Due Diligence:**

   - Have we conducted a thorough financial review of the target company?
   - Are there any potential regulatory issues or antitrust concerns?

- ○ Have we assessed the target's operational and human resources strengths and weaknesses?

3. **Governance and Leadership:**

- ○ Have we set clear roles for the board and management during the M&A process?
- ○ Are we empowering management to execute the deal while maintaining oversight?
- ○ Is there a clear integration plan with defined milestones?

4. **Post-Deal Integration:**

- ○ Have we developed a plan for integrating operations and culture?
- ○ Are there systems in place to monitor progress and address challenges?
- ○ Have we established a communication plan for stakeholders?

Key Takeaways & Summary

1. The board plays a critical role in overseeing M&A transactions, from setting the strategic rationale to ensuring effective integration.
2. Rigorous due diligence is essential to uncover potential risks and ensure that the deal aligns with the company's long-term strategy.
3. Clear governance, effective communication, and cultural integration are key to the success of M&A transactions.
4. Successful M&A examples, like ExxonMobil's merger, show how strategic alignment and strong leadership can transform companies, while unsuccessful transactions demonstrate the consequences of poor planning and execution.

For directors, the ability to assess and guide M&A decisions is a vital skill in corporate governance. With the right strategies in place, M&A

can be a powerful tool for growth and value creation, while also helping the company stay competitive in an ever-changing market. By following best practices and ensuring that both financial and cultural aspects are considered, directors can significantly improve the chances of a successful merger or acquisition.

Chapter 19

Capital Allocation

The Board's Role in Capital Allocation

Capital allocation is one of the most important functions of a board of directors. It involves making decisions about how a company's capital—whether sourced from equity, debt, or internal cash flow—is best deployed to maximise shareholder value. For directors, effective capital allocation means balancing risk and return while aligning investments with the long-term strategy of the organisation.

A board's capital allocation decisions have far-reaching implications on the company's growth trajectory, financial health, and market positioning. Poor capital allocation can lead to underperformance, missed opportunities, or financial distress, while sound decisions can lead to a competitive advantage, strong financial performance, and increased shareholder value.

At its core, capital allocation encompasses several areas: reinvestment in the business (organic growth), strategic acquisitions, dividend policies, share repurchases, and managing capital structure (debt vs. equity). In a world where capital is abundant but the choice of how to deploy it can be challenging, directors must ensure that decisions are made with a keen eye on both short-term and long-term goals.

This chapter explores the principles of sound capital allocation, the key factors directors should consider, and offers practical guidance for making informed investment decisions. We will also delve into a real-world case study that illustrates successful capital allocation and the lessons that can be learned from it.

Example: Amazon's Strategic Capital Allocation

Amazon's capital allocation strategy has been instrumental in its transformation from an online bookstore to one of the most valuable companies in the world. Unlike many companies that prioritise short-term shareholder returns through dividends or stock buybacks, Amazon has consistently reinvested its cash flow into long-term growth initiatives. This strategic approach, championed by founder and former CEO Jeff Bezos and supported by Amazon's board, underscores the importance of aligning capital allocation with a company's long-term vision.

Reinvestment in Core and Adjacent Businesses

Amazon has historically prioritised reinvestment over immediate returns to shareholders. The company allocated significant capital to build its robust infrastructure, such as its e-commerce platform, extensive logistics network, and customer-centric innovations like Prime membership. This reinvestment not only solidified its dominance in online retail but also enhanced customer loyalty and recurring revenue streams.

Additionally, Amazon diversified its capital deployment into adjacent businesses with high growth potential. For example, the company invested heavily in Amazon Web Services (AWS), which has become the leading cloud computing provider, contributing significantly to its overall profitability and market valuation.

Focus on R&D and Innovation

Amazon's board has consistently supported the company's high levels of spending on research and development (R&D) to maintain its competitive edge. Investments in artificial intelligence, machine learning, and automation have enabled innovations such as Alexa, its voice assistant, and drone delivery systems. These advancements have positioned Amazon as a technology leader while opening new revenue streams.

Disciplined Financial Management

While prioritising growth, Amazon maintained a disciplined approach to capital structure. The board and management worked together to balance investment needs with financial prudence, ensuring that debt levels remained manageable even during periods of aggressive expansion. This approach allowed the company to take calculated risks without jeopardising its financial stability.

Avoidance of Dividends and Buybacks

Amazon's decision not to distribute dividends or engage in stock buybacks reflects its commitment to reinvesting profits into the business. This strategy has resonated with long-term investors who value growth over short-term returns.

Outcomes and Lessons for Boards

'Amazon's capital allocation strategy has driven unparalleled growth and market leadership. By reinvesting profits into areas with the highest potential for long-term value creation, the company achieved extraordinary results. Its disciplined yet bold approach to deploying capital underscores several key lessons for boards:

1. **Prioritise Long-Term Growth:** Boards should align capital allocation decisions with the company's long-term strategy, even if it means delaying short-term returns.
2. **Diversify Investments:** Allocating capital to adjacent opportunities can create new growth engines while mitigating risk.
3. **Support Innovation:** Sustained investment in R&D is critical for maintaining a competitive edge and fostering future success.
4. **Exercise Financial Prudence:** Balancing ambitious investments with disciplined financial management ensures sustainable growth.

Practical Guidance for Directors: Best Practices in Capital Allocation

1. **Align Capital Allocation with Company Strategy:** A board should begin with a clear understanding of the company's strategic goals. Capital should be allocated in ways that support those goals, whether they involve organic growth, acquisitions, or maintaining a competitive edge through innovation. Investment decisions should not be made in isolation but should be closely tied to the company's overarching objectives.

2. **Focus on Return on Investment (ROI):** Directors should prioritise capital allocation decisions that generate the highest possible return relative to risk. Whether it is investing in new product development, making acquisitions, or expanding capacity, every allocation should be evaluated based on its expected ROI. Directors should also consider the time frame over which the return is expected, balancing short-term gains with long-term growth.

3. **Diversify the Capital Allocation Portfolio:** Diversification is a critical principle in capital allocation. Boards should allocate capital across various initiatives that complement each other and reduce reliance on any single project or investment. This could involve balancing spending on innovation and research, capital expenditures for growth, and maintaining cash reserves to cover unforeseen risks.

4. **Consider the Cost of Capital:** Understanding the cost of capital is essential when making investment decisions. Whether a company is financing a project with debt or equity, the cost of that capital affects the decision-making process. Boards should weigh the risks of taking on debt against the cost of equity and the return expected from the investment.

5. **Optimise the Capital Structure:** An important part of capital allocation is deciding how to finance investments. Boards should carefully consider the company's capital structure—how much debt versus equity is used—and ensure that it is optimised for the

company's risk profile and financial health. In some cases, taking on additional debt may make sense, while in others, reducing leverage may be the best course of action.

6. **Maintain Flexibility and Adaptability:** Capital allocation decisions should be revisited regularly as the business environment changes. Boards should be prepared to adapt their strategies based on new information, market conditions, or shifts in consumer demand. Flexibility is essential, particularly in volatile markets where long-term predictions can be uncertain.

7. **Ensure Transparency and Accountability:** For shareholders and stakeholders to have confidence in the board's decisions, transparency is key. Directors should ensure that capital allocation decisions are clearly communicated, with rationale and expected outcomes. Additionally, regular reporting on capital deployment and ROI is important to demonstrate accountability.

Table: Capital Allocation Decision-Making Framework

Step	Action
Strategic Alignment	Ensure investments align with long-term strategic objectives.
Risk Assessment	Evaluate risks associated with each potential investment.
Cost of Capital	Assess financing costs and expected returns from investment.
Return on Investment	Estimate ROI, factoring in both short-term and long-term returns.
Portfolio Diversification	Diversify investments across different initiatives to minimise risk.
Capital Structure Optimisation	Decide on the optimal mix of debt and equity for financing.
Flexibility & Adaptability	Be prepared to adjust strategy based on changing market conditions.

Interactive Element: Capital Allocation Quiz for Directors

Test Your Knowledge:

1. **What is the most critical factor to consider when allocating capital for a new project?**

    a) Short-term profits
    b) Alignment with long-term strategic goals
    c) Cost of labour
    d) Industry trends

2. **When considering debt financing for a new project, a director should:**

    a) Focus solely on minimising interest payments
    b) Assess the company's ability to service the debt while maintaining financial flexibility
    c) Only consider debt if equity financing is unavailable
    d) Avoid debt regardless of the potential return.

3. **In capital allocation, diversification is important because:**

    a) It reduces the risk of focusing on one project or market
    b) It always guarantees higher returns
    c) It reduces operational costs
    d) It simplifies the decision-making process

4. **What is the best way for a board to ensure it makes sound capital allocation decisions?**

    a) Make decisions based on past performance alone
    b) Regularly assess the strategic alignment of investments and returns
    c) Rely solely on senior management's recommendations
    d) Follow industry trends without analysis

Key Takeaways & Summary

1. **Capital Allocation is Crucial for Long-Term Success:** Effective capital allocation is essential for creating value and ensuring long-term growth. Directors must balance competing demands for capital, including reinvestment in the business, shareholder returns, and risk management.

2. **Case Study – Apple:** Apple's careful capital allocation, including returning cash to shareholders while reinvesting in growth opportunities, highlights the importance of strategic flexibility and long-term planning.

3. **Best Practices for Directors:** Directors should ensure that capital allocation aligns with the company's strategy, focuses on ROI, maintains a diversified portfolio, and optimises capital structure.

4. **Adaptability is Key:** Capital allocation decisions must be flexible and responsive to changing market conditions, requiring regular reassessment.

By following these principles and using a structured approach to evaluate and make capital allocation decisions, directors can enhance shareholder value and drive sustainable growth for their organisations. Top of Form

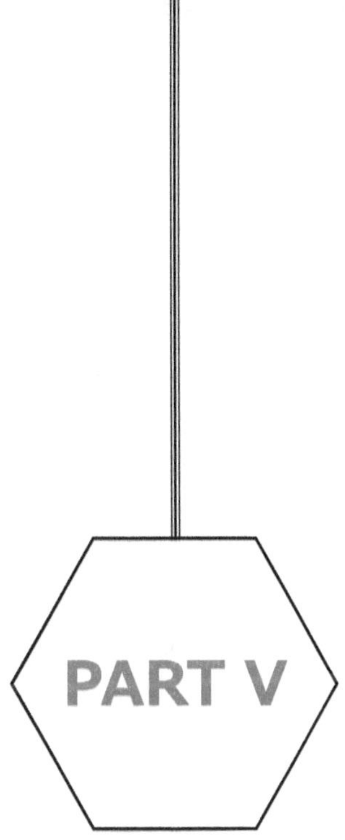

Board Meetings and Decision-Making

Chapter 20

Effective Board Meetings

Board meetings are the cornerstone of corporate governance. They serve as the platform where critical decisions are made, strategies are discussed, and the organisation's leadership is held accountable. The effectiveness of board meetings is not merely about having a group of experienced directors gather and discuss issues – it's about ensuring that these meetings are well-structured, purposeful, and result in informed, decisive action.

For directors, effective board meetings are vital to their role as stewards of the organisation. Through these meetings, the board can guide strategic direction, ensure financial integrity, manage risks, and oversee the execution of the company's goals. However, despite their importance, many boards struggle with inefficient meetings, which waste time, lack focus, and fail to address the core issues that require attention.

An effective board meeting is characterised by clear agendas, well-prepared directors, timely decision-making, and open communication. The goal is to foster an environment where the board can contribute meaningfully, engage in productive discussions, and make decisions that drive the organisation forward. This chapter will explore the best practices for planning and conducting board meetings, highlight a real-world example of successful meeting practices, and provide practical tips that will help directors lead more productive and efficient meetings.

Example: The Transformation of IBM's Board Meetings

A noteworthy example of effective board meetings comes from **IBM**, one of the world's largest and most innovative technology companies.

In the early 2000s, IBM faced significant challenges in adapting to the rapidly evolving tech landscape. The company's board meetings at the time were long, unproductive, and often bogged down in operational details rather than focusing on strategic vision.

In 2002, **Sam Palmisano** became the CEO of IBM, and he recognised the need for a change in how the company's board meetings were structured. Palmisano was determined to focus on high-level strategy, long-term goals, and the overarching direction of the company, rather than getting lost in minutiae. To make this shift, he restructured the board meetings by introducing a clear agenda, focusing on key strategic issues, and eliminating unnecessary updates that were irrelevant to the board's decision-making.

One major change was the introduction of pre-meeting briefings, where the board received detailed reports ahead of time, ensuring that everyone arrived at the meeting already informed. This allowed the meetings to focus on meaningful discussion and decision-making rather than spending time reviewing operational reports. Additionally, Palmisano encouraged a more interactive style of meetings, where directors felt comfortable challenging assumptions and proposing bold ideas.

As a result, IBM's board meetings became much more efficient and impactful. They were able to shift their focus from day-to-day operations to broader strategic discussions. This change in board governance helped IBM navigate the rapidly changing tech industry, culminating in a successful shift to software and services, which repositioned the company for long-term growth.

This example highlights the importance of structure and preparation in board meetings. By focusing on strategy, eliminating unnecessary details, and fostering open dialogue, 'IBM's board became more effective, ultimately steering the company through a period of profound transformation.

Practical Tips for Directors on Conducting Effective Board Meetings

Effective board meetings are the result of careful planning, clear objectives, and disciplined execution. Here are some practical tips for directors to ensure their board meetings are productive and result in meaningful decisions:

1. **Develop a Clear and Focused Agenda**

   A well-prepared agenda is the backbone of any effective board meeting. It sets the tone for the meeting, ensures that all critical topics are covered, and helps to manage time effectively. A good agenda should:

   - Prioritise strategic issues over routine updates.
   - Include specific discussion points for each agenda item.
   - Allocate time for each topic to prevent any one issue from dominating the meeting.

   o **Best Practice:** Send the agenda to directors well in advance (ideally a week before the meeting) to allow them to prepare adequately. Ensure the agenda is structured around the company's key strategic objectives and challenges.

2. **Establish a Pre-Meeting Briefing System**

   Provide directors with detailed reports and materials ahead of time so that they can come to the meeting informed and ready to engage in meaningful discussion. This reduces the time spent on updates during the meeting and ensures that the conversation can focus on decision-making and strategy.

   o **Best Practice:** Have management send reports on financial performance, key metrics, and strategic initiatives at least three to five days prior to the meeting. Directors should be encouraged to review these materials thoroughly before attending.

3.   **Limit Time on Operational Updates**

Board meetings are not meant to serve as management meetings. While important operational updates are necessary, they should be kept concise. Routine operational details should be provided in written reports that directors can review ahead of time.

- **Best Practice:** Dedicate only a small portion of the meeting (e. g. 10-15 minutes) for operational updates. Encourage management to focus on exceptions, risks, and significant changes, rather than presenting every detail.

4.   **Foster Open Communication and Discussion**

An effective board meeting should encourage open dialogue, where directors feel comfortable sharing their views, asking challenging questions, and proposing solutions. The board's role is to provide oversight, not just to approve decisions made by management. Directors should be empowered to actively contribute to discussions.

- **Best Practice:** Create an environment where dissent is welcomed. Encourage directors to ask tough questions and challenge assumptions, as this can lead to better decision-making and help identify potential risks early.

5.   **Use Decision-Making Tools and Frameworks**

Sometimes, discussions can become lengthy without yielding a clear decision. Implementing decision-making frameworks can help streamline discussions and bring clarity to the decision-making process. Tools like **SWOT analysis** (Strengths, Weaknesses, Opportunities, Threats) or **cost-benefit analysis** can provide a structured approach to evaluating options and making decisions.

- ○ **Best Practice:** Encourage the use of frameworks to evaluate major decisions. For instance, if the board is discussing a new business acquisition, use a cost-benefit analysis to weigh the pros and cons.

6. **Ensure Actionable Outcomes and Clear Follow-Ups**

At the end of each meeting, ensure that there are clear action items assigned to specific individuals, with deadlines for completion. This ensures that decisions made during the meeting lead to tangible outcomes and follow-through.

- ○ **Best Practice:** Use a "RACI" matrix (Responsible, Accountable, Consulted, and Informed) to assign roles for each action item. This helps ensure that everyone knows their responsibilities and is held accountable for delivering results.

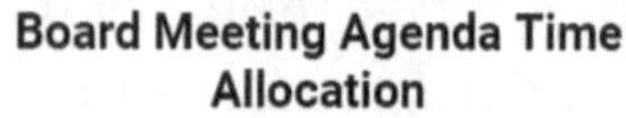

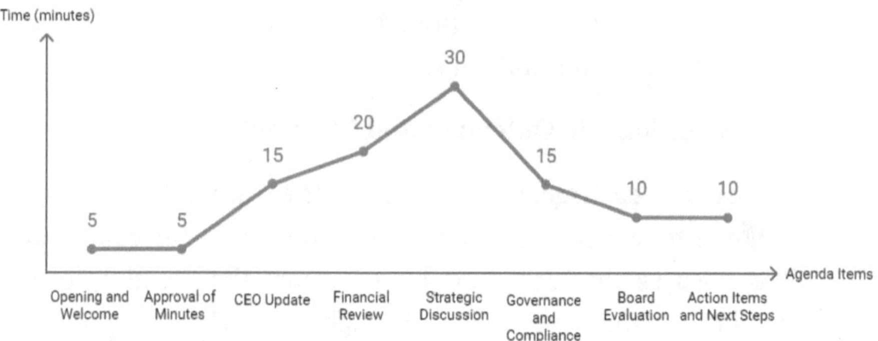

Interactive Element: Board Meeting Effectiveness Quiz

To help directors assess their meeting effectiveness, here's a quiz:

1. **Does your board meeting agenda focus on strategic issues rather than routine updates?**

   o   Yes / No / Sometimes

2. **Are all board members provided with detailed reports ahead of time?**

   o   Yes / No / Sometimes

3. **Does your board encourage open discussion and debate?**

   o   Yes / No / Sometimes

4. **Are action items assigned with clear responsibilities and deadlines?**

   o   Yes / No / Sometimes

5. **Does your board use decision-making frameworks to guide discussions?**

   o   Yes / No / Sometimes

Key Takeaways

1. **Preparation is Key:** Well-structured agendas and pre-meeting briefings ensure directors are informed and meetings stay focused.
2. **Strategic Focus:** Effective board meetings prioritise strategic decisions over routine updates.
3. **Encourage Open Dialogue:** Productive meetings require an open, respectful environment where directors can discuss issues candidly.
4. **Actionable Results:** Every meeting should end with clear decisions and action items that are followed up on.
5. **Evaluate Continuously:** Regular self-assessment of board effectiveness helps identify areas for improvement.

By incorporating these best practices, directors can transform board meetings from routine gatherings into powerful engines for governance and strategic decision-making.

Chapter 21

Board Materials

The Role of Well-Prepared Board Materials in Corporate Governance

One of the most critical factors influencing the effectiveness of a board of directors is the quality of the materials provided to them prior to board meetings. Board materials—such as reports, presentations, and supporting documents—are the tools through which directors stay informed, make decisions, and carry out their governance responsibilities. The quality of these materials directly impacts the board's ability to fulfil its role in overseeing the company's management, strategy, and operations.

Effective board materials provide the necessary information for directors to assess performance, evaluate risks, and make informed decisions. Whether a company is navigating financial challenges, undergoing a strategic pivot, or reviewing major capital investments, the board relies heavily on the clarity and relevance of the materials presented to them.

Inadequate or poorly prepared board materials can result in missed opportunities, inadequate oversight, and flawed decision-making, undermining the company's governance framework. Conversely, well-prepared materials help ensure that meetings are productive, that key issues are highlighted and discussed, and that decisions are made based on a comprehensive understanding of the company's operations and external environment.

This chapter will explore the importance of well-prepared board materials, provide examples of effective reports, and offer best practices and tips to help directors and company secretaries enhance the quality of board materials.

Example: The Role of Effective Board Materials in Tesla's Strategic Growth

A compelling example of the importance of effective board materials can be seen in Tesla's strategic growth in the electric vehicle (EV) market under CEO Elon Musk. During the early 2010s, Tesla faced significant challenges, including financial constraints, scaling production, and overcoming scepticism about the viability of EVs.

Key to navigating these challenges was the preparation of insightful, forward-looking board materials. 'Tesla's leadership presented the board with detailed reports that covered market trends, technological advancements, and the competitive landscape. These materials also included financial forecasts, production roadmaps, and scenario analyses that highlighted potential risks and rewards.

For instance, when Tesla planned to launch the Model 3—a car aimed at the mass market—comprehensive board materials helped directors understand the feasibility of scaling production while maintaining quality and managing costs. The board was equipped with data-driven insights, enabling them to engage in meaningful discussions, raise critical questions, and provide valuable guidance on funding strategies and operational priorities.

This approach fostered a culture of informed decision-making and alignment between the board and management, ultimately supporting Tesla's transformation from a niche automaker to a global leader in sustainable energy solutions.

The lesson from Tesla's journey is clear: well-prepared, actionable board materials can empower directors to provide strategic oversight and drive transformative change in an organisation.

Practical Guidance: Best Practices for Preparing Effective Board Materials

1. **Provide Clear and Concise Executive Summaries:** The board's time is limited, and directors need to quickly grasp the essential points of each topic. Executive summaries should highlight key findings, issues, and recommendations in a concise manner. These summaries should be tailored to the board's strategic oversight role, focusing on the big picture rather than getting lost in minutiae.

2. **Ensure Relevance and Strategic Focus:** Board materials should be aligned with the company's strategic priorities. Directors should not be bogged down with excessive detail that does not pertain to their decision-making responsibilities. For example, instead of providing a lengthy financial breakdown of every operational metric, materials should focus on key performance indicators (KPIs) that align with the company's strategic objectives.

3. **Use Data to Support Decision-Making:** Data-driven insights should form the backbone of board materials. Financial performance reports, risk assessments, and strategic proposals should be backed by clear, accurate, and up-to-date data. The use of visual aids—such as charts, graphs, and tables—can help directors digest complex data quickly.

4. **Anticipate Key Questions and Issues:** Effective board materials anticipate the questions or concerns that may arise during the meeting. Providing clear explanations of the company's challenges, opportunities, and potential risks enables directors to engage with the material more effectively. Including an "issues for discussion" section can guide directors on what they should be focusing on during the meeting.

5. **Ensure Transparency and Clarity:** Board materials should be transparent and straightforward. Avoid jargon, technical language, or overly complex explanations. If there is ambiguity

in any area, it is important to provide context and a clear explanation so that directors can make informed decisions.

6. **Allow Sufficient Time for Review:** Sending board materials well in advance of meetings is critical. Directors need time to thoroughly review the documents, ask questions, and prepare for the meeting. Typically, materials should be distributed at least 5–7 days before the meeting, depending on the complexity of the topics being discussed.

7. **Incorporate Actionable Recommendations:** Board materials should not just highlight issues but also provide actionable recommendations. Whether the recommendation is related to a strategic shift, an investment decision, or a governance issue, it should be clear, well-supported, and aligned with the company's goals. Directors should be able to understand the rationale behind the recommendation and the implications of their decisions.

Criteria	Yes	No	Comments
Executive Summary is clear and concise.			
The strategic relevance of the materials is evident.			
Data and metrics support the recommendations.			
Key risks and challenges are addressed.			
The tone and language are appropriate for directors.			
Materials are visually clear and easy to navigate.			
There is a clear call to action or decision point.			
Materials are sent with enough time for review.			

Interactive Element: Checklist for Reviewing Board Materials

Use the following checklist to evaluate the effectiveness of board materials:

Example of an Effective Board Report Structure:

Section	Content
1. Executive Summary	Key highlights, decisions required, and a brief overview of the topics covered.
2. Financial Performance	KPIs, income statement, balance sheet, and cash flow, along with an analysis of financial health.
3. Strategic Initiatives	Update on strategic projects, including timelines, milestones, and progress against objectives.
4. Risk Management	Overview of key risks, mitigation strategies, and contingency plans.
5. Governance and Compliance	Updates on compliance, governance issues, and regulatory changes affecting the company.
6. Issues for Discussion/ Decision	Areas where board input is needed, with options or recommendations clearly outlined.
7. Conclusion & Next Steps	Summary of decisions made, actions to be taken, and expected outcomes.

Key Takeaways & Summary

1. **Well-Prepared Materials Enable Effective Governance:** Board materials are essential tools for directors to make informed decisions, assess performance, and fulfil their oversight role. The quality of the materials can greatly influence the effectiveness of board meetings and the company's governance structure.

2. **Key Best Practices:** Directors should ensure that board materials are clear, relevant, data-driven, and aligned with the company's strategic goals. Materials should anticipate key questions and provide actionable recommendations.

3. **Transparency and Time Are Critical:** Materials must be transparent and free of ambiguity, and directors should receive them with enough time for a thorough review.

4. **Board Materials Structure:** An effective report structure includes an executive summary, financial performance data, strategic initiatives, risk management, and issues for discussion, making it easier for directors to focus on the most important topics.

By focusing on these best practices, boards can ensure that their decision-making processes are informed, efficient, and aligned with the company's long-term goals. Well-prepared materials are essential for effective corporate governance and play a critical role in the overall success of the organisation.

Chapter 22

Board Decision-Making

The Importance of Effective Decision-Making in Corporate Governance

Board decision-making is a crucial aspect of corporate governance. Boards are responsible for setting the strategic direction of the company, overseeing management's execution, and ensuring that the company is acting in the best interest of its stakeholders. Given the complexity and impact of their decisions, effective decision-making is not just about making the right call; it's about making decisions in a way that reflects the collective intelligence and diverse perspectives of the board.

Boards face a wide variety of decisions, ranging from approving budgets and executive compensation plans to overseeing mergers, acquisitions, and strategic pivots. In many cases, these decisions are made in high-pressure environments where the stakes are high, and the risks significant. This makes decision-making a critical skill that all directors must master.

In this chapter, we will explore the various techniques for group decision-making, the process of conflict resolution within boards, and real-world examples of how boards handle complex decisions. Effective decision-making is a collective process that requires transparency, communication, and careful consideration of all available data. Directors who are skilled in decision-making ensure that they are not only making the right decisions but doing so in a way that is ethical, transparent, and aligned with the company's long-term strategy.

Example: The Apple Board's Decision to Shift Strategy Under Tim Cook

One of the most well-known cases of successful board decision-making is Apple's shift under the leadership of Tim Cook. When Steve Jobs passed away in 2011, the board faced a monumental decision in choosing his successor. Apple's board not only had to decide on the right leadership transition but also on how to sustain Apple's market dominance amid increasing competition.

The board's decision to appoint Tim Cook was not just a matter of succession but also one of strategic pivot. Apple needed to expand its product lines and enter new markets, particularly in wearable tech and services. The board had to navigate a delicate balance between maintaining Apple's core culture and driving the company towards future growth. This involved extensive discussions, debates, and consultations with experts.

A key element in the board's decision-making process was the reliance on data and analysis. Cook's operational background, combined with Apple's impressive financial health, made him the right choice to execute Apple's evolving strategy. The board's decision to shift towards a focus on services, including the App Store, Apple Music, and iCloud, was another crucial decision for the company's long-term success.

This decision ultimately allowed Apple to diversify its revenue streams and thrive in a competitive environment, reinforcing the importance of careful, strategic decision-making at the board level.

Practical Guidance: Best Practices for Board Decision-Making

1. **Leverage Diverse Perspectives:** Effective decision-making in the boardroom requires input from a variety of perspectives. Directors often come from different backgrounds, industries, and

skill sets. Tapping into this diversity not only enhances creativity and innovation but also ensures that decisions are made with a broader understanding of potential impacts.

- o **Actionable Advice:** Encourage directors to challenge assumptions and bring forward alternative perspectives. Cultivate an environment where dissent is welcomed and viewed as a constructive tool for refining decisions.

2. **Data-Driven Decision-Making:** Decisions should be informed by data whenever possible. This can include financial reports, market trends, competitor analysis, and customer feedback. Having the right information at the right time is essential for making informed decisions that are aligned with the company's strategic objectives.

- o **Actionable Advice:** Implement systems to ensure that the board has access to the latest and most relevant data. Use visual tools like dashboards, charts, and graphs to present data in a clear and actionable manner.

3. **Establish Clear Decision-Making Processes:** Boards should have clear processes in place for making decisions, especially when those decisions are complex or high-stakes. This includes setting clear criteria for evaluating options, ensuring that all relevant stakeholders are consulted, and using structured approaches like voting or consensus-building when appropriate.

- o **Actionable Advice:** Develop a standardised decision-making framework that all directors understand and follow. This framework can include timelines, responsible parties, and steps for resolution.

4. **Facilitate Open Communication and Dialogue:** Decision-making is most effective when directors can openly discuss options, voice

concerns, and share their perspectives. This requires a culture of transparency and respect, where directors feel comfortable speaking up.

- o **Actionable Advice:** Foster an environment that encourages open communication. Use tools like "round-robin" discussions or structured debates to ensure everyone has a chance to contribute their ideas.

5. **Address and Resolve Conflicts Constructively:** Conflicts in the boardroom are inevitable, especially when it comes to complex or controversial decisions. How the board handles these conflicts can make a significant difference in the quality of the decision and the board's cohesion.

- o **Actionable Advice:** When conflict arises, use structured conflict resolution techniques such as active listening, negotiation, and mediation. Encourage directors to focus on the issue at hand rather than personalities, and try to reach a consensus or a vote when necessary.

6. **Accountability and Follow-Through:** Once decisions are made, it's important for the board to ensure that they are implemented effectively. This involves setting up mechanisms for accountability and reviewing progress against agreed-upon outcomes.

- o **Actionable Advice:** Establish clear action items and timelines for implementation. Regularly check in on the progress of decisions to ensure accountability.

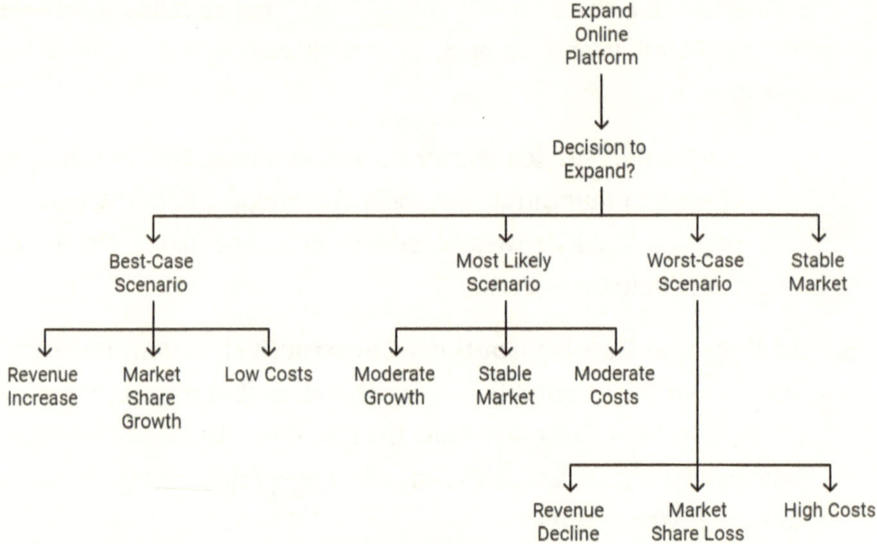

Interactive Element: Discussion Question

Scenario: The board of a large retail company is debating whether to invest in expanding its online platform to compete with a new e-commerce giant. The CEO is advocating for the expansion, while several board members are concerned about the risk, the cost, and the potential return on investment. The discussion is becoming increasingly polarised.

Discussion Question:

- How can the board resolve this conflict effectively while ensuring that the decision is based on data and aligned with the company's long-term strategy? What techniques could be used to facilitate open communication and ensure that all viewpoints are considered?

Key Takeaways & Summary

- **Effective Decision-Making is Key to Corporate Governance:** Board decision-making is a critical function in corporate governance. Well-executed decisions ensure that a company stays on track with its strategy, adapts to changing circumstances, and meets the needs of stakeholders.

- **Diverse Perspectives and Data-Driven Insights Lead to Better Outcomes:** Incorporating diverse viewpoints and basing decisions on solid data helps the board make informed, strategic choices that will have long-term benefits.

- **Clear Processes and Open Communication are Essential:** Establishing decision-making frameworks, encouraging open communication, and resolving conflicts constructively can help boards make decisions efficiently and with a strong sense of unity.

- **Accountability Ensures Effective Implementation:** Once a decision is made, tracking its progress and ensuring follow-through are crucial for the success of the decision and the board's overall effectiveness.

By utilising these techniques, boards can navigate even the most complex decisions with confidence and ensure that their company is on the path to long-term success.

Chapter 23

Board Evaluations

Board evaluations are a cornerstone of effective corporate governance. They provide an opportunity for directors to assess their performance, identify areas for improvement, and strengthen the overall effectiveness of the board. The goal of a board evaluation is not merely to judge individual performance but to evaluate the collective functionality of the board, its committees, and its interaction with the executive team. When conducted correctly, these evaluations lead to better decision-making, improved governance practices, and more strategic leadership.

For directors, board evaluations are a crucial aspect of their fiduciary responsibility. They ensure that the board is fulfilling its role effectively, overseeing the management team properly, and adhering to its governance obligations. In an ever-evolving business environment, where expectations for corporate responsibility and performance are higher than ever, conducting regular and meaningful board evaluations is vital for maintaining credibility and achieving long-term success.

This chapter will explore how to conduct meaningful board evaluations, the types of evaluations available, best practices, and practical tips for directors to ensure they extract maximum value from the evaluation process. We will also include templates and sample questions that can help guide the process.

Example: The Role of Board Evaluations in the Revitalisation of Coca-Cola

A compelling example of the transformative power of board evaluations comes from Coca-Cola during the early 2010s. Facing slowing growth in its core carbonated beverage business and increasing consumer demand for healthier alternatives, Coca-Cola needed to rethink its strategy to stay competitive.

Under the leadership of then-CEO Muhtar Kent, the company initiated a comprehensive evaluation of its board. This process included assessing the board's composition, identifying gaps in expertise, and evaluating its ability to guide the company through a period of significant change. One of the key findings from this evaluation was the need for more directors with backgrounds in nutrition, emerging markets, and digital marketing to help Coca-Cola expand its portfolio and connect with a new generation of consumers.

In response, Coca-Cola revamped its board by bringing in directors with diverse experiences and global perspectives. The newly structured board provided the company with insights to navigate shifting consumer preferences, leading to a stronger focus on low-sugar and zero-calorie drinks, as well as investments in non-carbonated beverages like water, tea, and sports drinks.

This renewed board oversight also strengthened Coca-Cola's sustainability initiatives, with a focus on reducing packaging waste and improving water management—areas increasingly important to consumers and regulators.

The Coca-Cola case highlights how board evaluations can identify critical gaps, enhance strategic decision-making, and enable companies to adapt to changing market demands. By aligning its board's expertise with its evolving business strategy, Coca-Cola was able to secure its position as a leader in the beverage industry.

Practical Tips and Best Practices for Conducting Board Evaluations

Board evaluations are most effective when they are conducted regularly, thoughtfully, and with a focus on continuous improvement.

The following best practices can help ensure that evaluations are meaningful and lead to actionable outcomes:

1. **Set Clear Objectives for the Evaluation**

    Before initiating any evaluation process, it is crucial to define the purpose and objectives. Are you evaluating the performance of the entire board, individual directors, or specific committees? What aspects of governance or board dynamics are you trying to assess? By setting clear objectives, you ensure that the evaluation will be focused and aligned with the organisation's needs.

    o   **Best Practice:** Ensure that the evaluation process is aligned with the company's overall strategy and goals. This way, the insights gathered from the evaluation can directly inform the company's future direction.

2. **Choose the Right Evaluation Format**

    There are various methods for conducting board evaluations, including:

    *   **Self-Evaluation:** Directors assess their own performance and the board's effectiveness through questionnaires or interviews.
    *   **Peer Evaluation:** Directors evaluate the performance of their fellow board members, typically focusing on collaboration, leadership, and contribution to discussions.
    *   **External Evaluation:** An independent third party (such as an external consultant) conducts the evaluation, providing an unbiased assessment of the board's effectiveness.

    Each method has its advantages. Self-evaluations are often the most straightforward, but they can lack objectivity. Peer evaluations can provide insight into individual dynamics but may be influenced by personal relationships. External evaluations provide an objective perspective, but they can be costly.

- o **Best Practice:** A hybrid approach—using self and peer evaluations followed by an external consultant's feedback—can provide a well-rounded assessment.

3. **Ensure Confidentiality and Transparency**

For board evaluations to be effective, directors must feel comfortable sharing candid feedback. This can only happen in a climate of trust, where feedback is kept confidential. Ensure that the process is designed to protect the anonymity of responses, especially when it comes to peer evaluations.

- o **Best Practice:** If conducting an internal evaluation, appoint an independent committee or use a third-party consultant to collect and analyse feedback. This ensures confidentiality and fosters openness.

4. **Analyse Results and Follow Through**

Once the evaluation data is collected, it is essential to analyse the results and identify trends or areas for improvement. The findings should be presented to the board in a constructive way, focusing on both strengths and weaknesses.

- o **Best Practice:** The board should discuss the results openly, prioritising actionable improvements. The findings should inform future board development plans, such as training programmes, changes to the board structure, or adjustments to the governance processes.

5. **Make Evaluations an Ongoing Process**

Board evaluations should not be a one-off event. To be truly effective, evaluations need to be part of an ongoing process of self-improvement. Incorporate follow-up evaluations and track progress over time. This will allow the board to continuously refine its processes and adapt to changing needs.

- ○ **Best Practice:** Make evaluations a regular part of the board's calendar. For example, conduct a full board evaluation every 1-2 years, with more focused evaluations (such as committee performance or individual contributions) conducted annually.

Sample Board Evaluation Template

Below is a simple template that can be used as part of a board evaluation process. This template focuses on evaluating the overall effectiveness of the board, individual directors, and the performance of committees.

Table: Sample Evaluation Questions for Board Members

Topic	Question	Rating Scale
Board Leadership	Does the Chairperson facilitate effective meetings?	1-5 (1 = Poor, 5 = Excellent)
Board Dynamics	Are discussions open and respectful?	1-5 (1 = Poor, 5 = Excellent)
Committee Performance	Are committees effectively fulfilling their roles?	1-5 (1 = Poor, 5 = Excellent)
Director Engagement	Does the director actively participate in meetings?	1-5 (1 = Poor, 5 = Excellent)

Board Effectiveness Evaluation

1. **Board Leadership**

   - ○ Does the board provide effective leadership to the organisation? (Yes/No)
   - ○ Does the Chairperson facilitate productive board discussions? (Yes/No)
   - ○ Does the board have a clear understanding of its role and responsibilities? (Yes/No)

2. **Board Composition and Skills**

   ○ Does the board have the right mix of skills and experience to meet the company's needs? (Yes/No)
   ○ Is there sufficient diversity in terms of gender, ethnicity, and professional backgrounds? (Yes/No)

3. **Board Dynamics**

   ○ Is there open and respectful communication among board members? (Yes/No)
   ○ Are board members engaged in the decision-making process? (Yes/No)
   ○ Does the board foster a culture of constructive debate? (Yes/No)

4. **Committee Performance**

   ○ Does each board committee have a clear mandate and objectives? (Yes/No)
   ○ Are committees effectively supporting the board in its oversight role? (Yes/No)

5. **Overall Board Performance**

   ○ Does the board effectively oversee the company's strategy? (Yes/No)
   ○ Does the board monitor management's performance and hold them accountable? (Yes/No)

Director Evaluation

- **Contribution to Board Meetings:**

   ○ Does the director actively contribute to discussions? (Yes/No)

- Does the director provide valuable insights based on their expertise? (Yes/No)

- **Engagement and Commitment:**

    - Does the director attend meetings regularly? (Yes/No)
    - Does the director stay informed about the company's performance and strategy? (Yes/No)

Committee Evaluation

- **Committee Leadership:**

    - Is the committee chair effective in guiding discussions and making decisions? (Yes/No)
    - Are the committee's activities aligned with the company's strategic goals? (Yes/No)

- **Committee Collaboration:**

    - Does the committee work collaboratively with management and the board? (Yes/No)

Enhancing Board Performance

Follow-up

Conduct periodic evaluations to track progress.

Action Plan

Create a plan to address issues and improve performance.

Analysis

Identify strengths and areas for improvement.

Data Collection

Gather feedback through surveys and interviews.

Planning

Establish clear objectives and methods for evaluation.

Interactive Element: Discussion Questions for the Board

To engage directors in the evaluation process, here are some thought-provoking questions to consider:

1. How can we improve communication and collaboration among board members?
2. Are there areas of governance where we feel underprepared, and how can we address this?
3. What skills or expertise do we need to add to the board to improve decision-making?
4. How do we handle conflict within the board, and can we improve this process?
5. What steps can we take to make our board meetings more effective and focused on strategic issues?

Key Takeaways

1. Board evaluations are an essential tool for maintaining effective governance and ensuring that boards remain aligned with the strategic goals of the organisation.
2. A well-executed evaluation provides insights into the board's strengths and areas for improvement, driving continuous improvement in governance practices.
3. Regular evaluations, combined with follow-up action plans, foster a culture of accountability, transparency, and performance-driven leadership.
4. Directors should use board evaluations as a platform for constructive feedback, both for individual directors and the board as a whole.

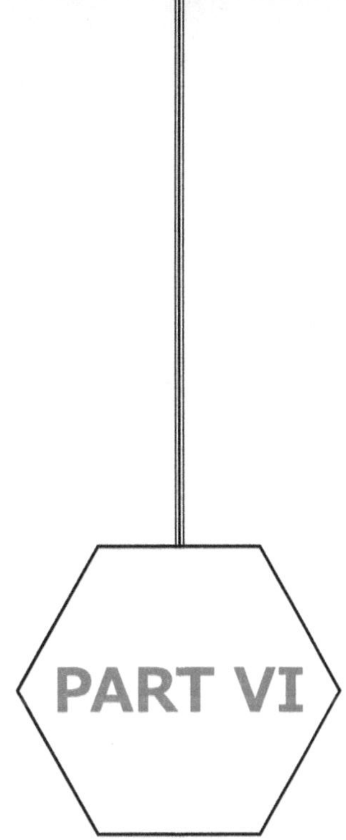

Challenges and Opportunities

Chapter 24

Emerging Issues in Corporate Governance

Corporate governance is evolving rapidly in the face of new challenges and opportunities, driven by global economic shifts, technological advancements, and heightened societal expectations. Historically, corporate governance emphasised financial transparency, accountability, and shareholder interests. Today, however, boards must grapple with a broader range of issues, from Environmental, Social, and Governance (ESG) concerns to the increasingly critical domain of cybersecurity. These areas are now central to business success and sustainability.

Emerging challenges are redefining the role of corporate boards, requiring directors to oversee not only traditional financial risks but also complex issues like corporate responsibility, environmental stewardship, and data security. Investors, regulators, and consumers are pressing companies to act responsibly, sustainably, and securely. Boards must proactively adapt and develop strategies to manage these issues effectively.

This chapter will delve into two key emerging issues in corporate governance—ESG and cybersecurity—and explore how companies are addressing these challenges. It will include real-world examples, best practices for directors, and tools to help boards navigate an increasingly complex governance landscape.

Example: The SolarWinds Cybersecurity Breach

One of the most pressing governance challenges in recent years has been cybersecurity, underscored by the 2020 SolarWinds cyberattack.

SolarWinds, a U.S.-based IT management company, became the target of a sophisticated supply chain attack that compromised its Orion software. The breach, which went undetected for months, allowed hackers—believed to be state-sponsored actors—to infiltrate the networks of thousands of organisations, including major corporations and U.S. government agencies.

This event highlighted the far-reaching impact of cyber risks, demonstrating that even companies with a strong technological foundation are vulnerable. The attack served as a wake-up call for corporate boards to prioritise cybersecurity as a strategic governance issue.

SolarWinds' Response and Governance Lessons:

In the wake of the breach, SolarWinds implemented several governance measures to address cybersecurity risks and restore trust:

1. **Strengthening Board-Level Oversight:**

   SolarWinds established a dedicated cybersecurity committee within its board of directors to ensure direct and continuous oversight of cyber risks. This move signalled a commitment to integrating cybersecurity into the company's governance framework.

2. **Leadership Accountability:**

   The company appointed a Chief Information Security Officer (CISO) with a direct reporting line to the board. This structure ensured transparency and emphasised cybersecurity as a top priority at the executive and board levels.

3. **Adopting Zero-Trust Principles:**

   SolarWinds transitioned to a "zero-trust" security model, which assumes that no user or system can be inherently trusted. This proactive approach involved implementing advanced identity verification and data protection protocols.

4. **Engaging External Experts:**

SolarWinds collaborated with cybersecurity experts, law enforcement, and regulatory bodies to investigate the breach and enhance its defences. This partnership helped the company regain credibility and rebuild stakeholder confidence.

5. **Enhanced Communication with Stakeholders:**

The board prioritised transparent communication about the breach, its implications, and the steps being taken to prevent future incidents. This openness was critical in rebuilding trust with customers, investors, and regulators.

Outcome and Broader Implications:

The SolarWinds breach was a turning point for cybersecurity governance across industries. While the company faced initial reputational and financial setbacks, its commitment to addressing the root causes of the attack and enhancing governance practices has been a model for other organisations. Boards worldwide have since recognised the importance of robust cybersecurity oversight, emphasising preparedness, accountability, and transparency.

Emerging Issues in Governance: ESG (Environmental, Social, and Governance)

While cybersecurity risks are critical, the rise of **ESG (Environmental, Social, and Governance)** factors has emerged as one of the most significant challenges and opportunities in corporate governance today. ESG concerns address how companies impact the environment, society, and the broader governance landscape.

Why ESG Matters to Boards

In the past decade, ESG has gained significant traction among investors, regulators, and consumers. Stakeholders are increasingly holding companies accountable not just for financial performance but also for how they impact the world around them. Directors must ensure that ESG considerations are integrated into their business strategy, risk management processes, and decision-making frameworks.

For example, **BlackRock**, the world's largest asset manager, has made ESG a cornerstone of its investment strategy. Larry Fink, the company's CEO, has written several annual letters to CEOs, urging them to prioritise long-term sustainable growth and provide detailed reporting on their ESG activities. As a result, many companies have ramped up their efforts to address climate change, social responsibility, and governance practices, often aligning their strategies with global frameworks such as the United Nations' Sustainable Development Goals (SDGs).

Real-World Example: Unilever and ESG Integration

Unveiling Corporate Governance Dimensions

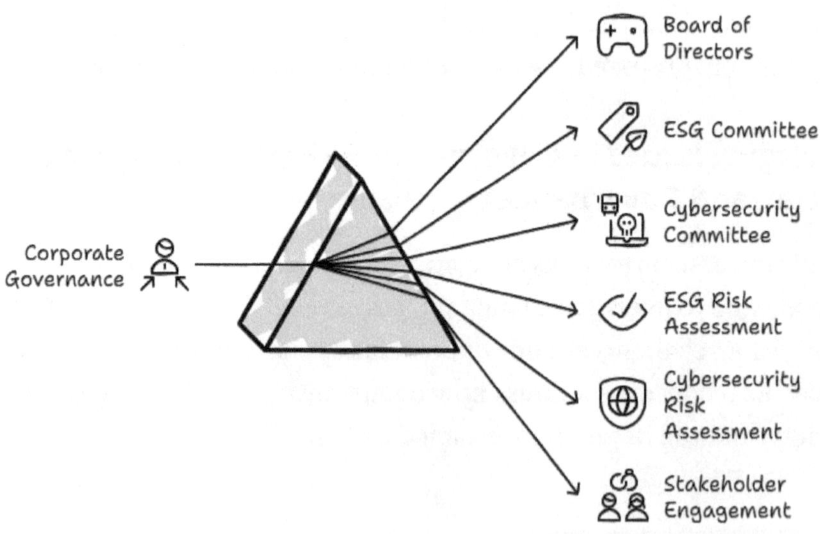

Unilever, a multinational consumer goods company, provides an excellent example of how integrating ESG into corporate governance can drive long-term value creation. Under the leadership of former CEO Paul Polman, Unilever committed to making sustainability a core part of its business strategy.

Unilever's **Sustainable Living Plan**, launched in 2010, set ambitious targets to reduce the company's environmental footprint, improve health and well-being for people around the world, and enhance the livelihoods of those in its supply chain. The company's governance model evolved to include more robust ESG oversight, with board members actively involved in setting sustainability goals, assessing risks, and monitoring progress.

In 2020, Unilever set a target to achieve **net-zero emissions by 2039**, addressing the growing concerns about climate change and its impact on business operations. The company also focused on improving diversity, equity, and inclusion, with the board overseeing these efforts to ensure that Unilever maintained a responsible and transparent approach to ESG matters.

Unilever's dedication to ESG principles has not only improved its environmental and social impact but has also bolstered its brand reputation, attracting investors and consumers who prioritise sustainability. This case underscores the importance of integrating ESG into corporate governance and demonstrates how doing so can lead to long-term success.

Practical Tips for Directors on Managing Emerging Issues

As ESG and cybersecurity challenges become more pressing, it's essential that boards adopt best practices to address these risks proactively. Below are some practical tips for directors on managing these emerging issues:

1. **Establish Clear Governance Frameworks for ESG and Cybersecurity**

Boards should establish dedicated committees or subcommittees for ESG and cybersecurity oversight. These committees should report directly to the board to ensure that these issues are considered at the highest level of governance. Furthermore, the board should ensure that its governance frameworks are aligned with global standards and frameworks, such as the **Task Force on Climate-related Financial Disclosures (TCFD)** for ESG or the **National Institute of Standards and Technology (NIST)** framework for cybersecurity.

2. **Enhance Stakeholder Engagement**

Engagement with a range of stakeholders—investors, customers, employees, and regulators—is critical for understanding their concerns and expectations on ESG and cybersecurity issues. Directors should ensure that their companies actively engage in dialogue on these topics and prioritise transparency in their reporting practices.

3. **Foster a Culture of Cybersecurity Awareness**

Given the increasing sophistication of cyberattacks, boards should foster a culture of cybersecurity awareness throughout the organisation. This includes investing in training programmes for employees, promoting cybersecurity best practices, and ensuring that adequate resources are allocated to cybersecurity efforts.

4. **Monitor ESG and Cybersecurity Risks as Part of Enterprise Risk Management**

Boards should include ESG and cybersecurity risks in their overall **enterprise risk management (ERM)** framework.

Directors should regularly review risk assessments and ensure that appropriate mitigation strategies are in place.

5. **Set Measurable Goals and Track Progress**

    Both ESG and cybersecurity initiatives should be tracked with measurable goals, clear timelines, and performance metrics. Boards must ensure that the company is making tangible progress in these areas and that there is accountability for achieving the set targets.

Table: Key ESG Reporting Frameworks

Framework	Key Focus Areas	Stakeholders
TCFD (Task Force on Climate-related Financial Disclosures)	Climate-related risks, opportunities, and financial impact	Investors, Regulators
GRI (Global Reporting Initiative)	Broader sustainability goals, social impact, and environmental performance	Consumers, NGOs, Investors
SASB (Sustainability Accounting Standards Board)	Industry-specific ESG metrics for financial reporting	Investors, Regulators
NIST Cybersecurity Framework	Cybersecurity risk management practices	Boards, IT teams, Regulators

Interactive Element: Discussion Questions for the Board

To engage directors in thinking about the emerging issues of ESG and cybersecurity, consider these discussion questions:

1. How does our current governance framework address ESG and cybersecurity risks? Are there areas for improvement?
2. What steps can we take to integrate sustainability more deeply into our business strategy and operations?
3. How can we enhance the company's cybersecurity posture in response to growing external threats?

4. Are we engaging with stakeholders on ESG issues in a meaningful way? What more can we do to improve transparency?

5. How do we balance the short-term financial performance of the company with long-term sustainability goals?

Key Takeaways

1. Emerging issues such as ESG and cybersecurity are reshaping the landscape of corporate governance.

2. Directors must establish clear governance frameworks and strategies to address these emerging risks.

3. Proactive engagement with stakeholders, robust risk management, and continuous monitoring are key to navigating these challenges effectively.

4. Companies that integrate ESG principles and cybersecurity measures into their business strategies position themselves for long-term success while fostering stakeholder trust and resilience in a rapidly changing world.

Chapter 25

The Impact of Technology

The Role of Technology in Enhancing Board Effectiveness

In today's rapidly evolving business landscape, technology is no longer a luxury; it's an essential tool for driving growth, innovation, and operational efficiency. For boards of directors, embracing the right technologies can greatly enhance decision-making, streamline processes, and improve overall governance. As companies are faced with increasing pressures to act swiftly and responsibly, technology can provide the tools to help boards operate more effectively, transparently, and strategically.

The digital age has introduced a range of technological tools that help directors meet the growing demands of their roles, from ensuring compliance to overseeing strategy execution. Tools like board portals, analytics software, and AI are now becoming critical components of modern board governance. These tools enable boards to access real-time information, collaborate more efficiently, and monitor performance more accurately.

In this chapter, we will explore the various ways technology enhances board effectiveness. We will also examine real-world examples of companies leveraging technology for improved governance, as well as provide actionable insights for directors to implement technology tools effectively within their own boards.

Example: The Use of Board Portals at Adidas

Adidas, a global leader in sportswear, provides an excellent example of how technology can enhance board governance. In recent years, the company adopted a digital board portal to modernise its communication and decision-making processes. Previously, Adidas's board relied on extensive printed materials for meetings, which were often cumbersome and led to delays in disseminating critical information.

With the implementation of a secure digital board portal, Adidas' directors now have instant access to meeting agendas, strategic reports, financial data, and other critical documents. The portal enables directors to review materials well in advance, annotate documents, and pose questions directly to management, fostering more productive and focused board discussions.

Additionally, the board portal supports secure voting and digital signatures, expediting decision-making processes while maintaining compliance and transparency. The technology also proved invaluable in facilitating seamless collaboration among board members located in different regions, ensuring that Adidas' governance kept pace with the demands of its global operations.

By integrating digital tools into its governance framework, Adidas has enhanced its operational efficiency and fostered better collaboration at the board level. This technological shift underscores the importance of adapting governance practices to meet the challenges of a rapidly changing, competitive global market.

Practical Guidance: How Technology Enhances Board Effectiveness

1. **Board Portals: Streamlining Communication and Document Management**

   Board portals are secure online platforms designed specifically for board communication. They offer a centralised location where directors can access meeting materials, financial reports, compliance documents, and other key information. With features such as version control, real-time collaboration, and secure document sharing, board portals reduce the inefficiencies associated with traditional paper-based processes.

- o **Actionable Advice:** Boards should invest in secure, user-friendly board portals that ensure the safe and efficient sharing of sensitive documents. Directors should be trained on how to use these tools to maximise their benefits, particularly when it comes to reviewing materials and collaborating before meetings.

2. **Analytics Software: Empowering Data-Driven Decision-Making**

In today's data-driven world, analytics software plays a vital role in helping boards make informed decisions. These tools aggregate vast amounts of data from various sources and present it in easily interpretable formats such as charts, graphs, and dashboards. This enables directors to access key performance indicators (KPIs) and other metrics in real-time, providing them with valuable insights to guide their decision-making processes.

- o **Actionable Advice:** Directors should encourage the use of analytics software to track performance across various areas of the business, such as financial health, customer satisfaction, and operational efficiency. Regular reviews of performance metrics will enable the board to take corrective actions in a timely manner.

3. **AI and Machine Learning: Improving Risk Management and Forecasting**

AI and machine learning technologies have revolutionised the way companies approach risk management and forecasting. AI-powered tools can analyse patterns in large datasets to predict future trends, detect anomalies, and identify potential risks. This is particularly useful for boards overseeing complex global operations where risk management is crucial.

- Actionable Advice: Boards should explore AI-based tools for risk identification and mitigation. These technologies can be used to track market trends, identify emerging risks, and forecast future financial performance, allowing the board to make more informed and proactive decisions.

4. **Cybersecurity Tools: Safeguarding Board Data and Company Assets**

As boards rely more on digital tools, the importance of robust cybersecurity measures cannot be overstated. Board members often handle sensitive company information, including financial data, intellectual property, and strategic plans. Ensuring that this data is secure from cyber threats is critical to maintaining trust and confidentiality.

- Actionable Advice: Boards must prioritise cybersecurity by investing in advanced tools to protect their digital platforms. Regular audits of cybersecurity systems and training for directors on how to recognise potential security threats are essential to mitigating risks associated with digital vulnerabilities.

5. **Video Conferencing and Collaboration Tools: Facilitating Remote and Hybrid Meetings**

The COVID-19 pandemic accelerated the adoption of video conferencing tools such as Zoom, Microsoft Teams, and Google Meet. These tools have become an essential part of board governance, allowing directors to participate in meetings remotely or in a hybrid format. They also facilitate real-time collaboration and decision-making across geographies.

- Actionable Advice: Boards should incorporate video conferencing tools to ensure flexibility in meeting participation. This is especially important for global organisations with directors located in various regions. Boards should also establish guidelines for effective virtual meetings, ensuring that all members have equal opportunities to participate.

6. **Cloud-Based Solutions: Ensuring Seamless Access to Board Materials**

Cloud-based platforms provide directors with access to board materials, financial reports, and other important documents anytime, anywhere. These solutions eliminate the need for physical document storage and allow directors to review and collaborate on materials in real-time.

- **Actionable Advice:** Implement cloud-based solutions to ensure that directors have uninterrupted access to essential materials. Ensure that cloud services comply with industry standards for data protection and security.

Interactive Element: Technology Adoption Checklist

Checklist: Is Your Board Ready to Leverage Technology?

- Do you have a secure digital board portal in place for sharing documents and communication?
- Are you using analytics tools to track KPIs and make data-driven decisions?
- Has the board explored AI-powered solutions for risk management and forecasting?
- Are there established cybersecurity protocols in place to protect sensitive data?
- Is the board utilising video conferencing tools for remote or hybrid meetings?
- Have you implemented cloud-based platforms for seamless access to materials?

Discussion Question:

- How can boards ensure that they are selecting and implementing the right technologies for their unique needs? What are the most critical factors to consider when adopting new technologies for governance?

Key Takeaways & Summary

1. **Technology Drives Efficiency and Transparency:** The adoption of technology can significantly enhance a board's efficiency by streamlining communication, enabling real-time collaboration, and providing secure access to essential materials.

2. **Data-driven Decision-making is Essential:** Tools like analytics software and AI empower boards to make informed decisions based on real-time data, thereby improving the quality and speed of decision-making.

3. **Cybersecurity and Security Measures Are Critical:** As boards rely more on digital tools, ensuring the security of sensitive information becomes paramount. Boards should prioritise cybersecurity to protect company data and maintain trust.

4. **Adaptability to Remote and Hybrid Environments:** The use of video conferencing and cloud-based solutions allows for flexible and inclusive board meetings, ensuring that all directors can participate regardless of location.

By leveraging the right technologies, boards can not only enhance their operational effectiveness but also future-proof their governance structures in a rapidly changing business environment. Directors must be proactive in embracing these tools to stay ahead of emerging challenges and capitalise on new opportunities.

Chapter 26

Crisis Management

The Board's Role in Crisis Management

Crisis management is an essential skill for any board of directors, as it can define the future of a company. The ability to respond to a crisis with clarity, decisive action, and strategic foresight can either preserve a company's reputation and viability or contribute to its downfall. In today's fast-paced and interconnected business environment, crises can arise unexpectedly, from financial downturns, public relations disasters, and regulatory challenges to operational failures, cybersecurity breaches, or global pandemics.

For boards, crisis management goes beyond damage control. It requires a proactive approach to identifying potential risks, preparing response strategies, and executing them swiftly and efficiently when needed. Directors must manage the immediate impact of a crisis while also planning for long-term recovery and adaptation, which is critical to shaping the company's future.

In this chapter, we will explore the board's critical role during crises, the importance of maintaining calm and control, and the steps directors can take to help their companies navigate turbulent times. A real-world example will illustrate how good crisis management can determine an organisation's survival and success, offering practical advice for directors on preparing for and handling crises effectively.

Example: Boeing 737 MAX Crisis

A notable example of crisis management and the challenges of inadequate response is the Boeing 737 MAX crisis. In 2018 and

2019, two separate crashes involving Boeing 737 MAX airplanes (Lion Air Flight 610 and Ethiopian Airlines Flight 302) tragically claimed 346 lives. Investigations revealed that a malfunction in the aircraft's Manoeuvring Characteristics Augmentation System (MCAS) contributed to both accidents. The fallout from these events quickly escalated into one of the most significant crises in aviation history.

The crisis tested Boeing's leadership and governance. The company faced a global grounding of the 737 MAX fleet, widespread scrutiny from regulators, lawmakers, and the public, and significant financial and reputational damage.

Board Response and Crisis Management Efforts

Boeing's response provides key lessons in crisis management—both in terms of what worked and what fell short:

1. **Initial Communication Missteps:**

   In the early stages of the crisis, Boeing struggled with public perception, as its initial responses were perceived as defensive and lacking empathy for the victims and their families. This highlighted the importance of clear and compassionate communication during a crisis.

2. **Re-evaluation of Leadership:**

   The crisis led to significant changes in Boeing's leadership, including the removal of the CEO, as the board sought to rebuild trust with stakeholders and emphasise accountability.

3. **Commitment to Transparency:**

   Boeing's board eventually acknowledged the need for transparency and began cooperating more openly with regulators and investigators. They committed to overhauling safety processes and enhancing the role of safety experts in decision-making.

4. **Financial Recovery Measures:**

The crisis cost Boeing billions in lost revenue, legal settlements, and penalties. The board approved measures to manage the financial impact, including suspending share buybacks and raising new capital to stabilise the company's finances.

5. **Long-Term Cultural Change:**

One of the most critical board-driven initiatives was addressing the company's internal culture, which had been criticised for prioritising speed-to-market over safety. The board worked to reinforce a safety-first ethos throughout the organisation.

Visualizing Crisis Management Steps

Outcomes and Governance Lessons

While Boeing's response faced significant criticism, the company has made progress in rebuilding trust and enhancing its safety culture. The 737 MAX was eventually recertified for flight after extensive reviews, and Boeing has worked to implement governance reforms that prioritise safety and accountability.

Key Takeaways for Boards

The Boeing crisis underscores the importance of several principles in crisis management:

- **Empathy and Communication:** Boards must ensure that the company communicates with compassion, transparency, and humility during crises.
- **Accountability:** Boards must hold leadership accountable and make bold decisions to address systemic issues, even if it involves leadership changes.
- **Proactive Risk Management:** A culture of safety, compliance, and risk mitigation must be ingrained in corporate governance to prevent crises from occurring.
- **Strategic Recovery Planning:** Boards must focus on long-term recovery strategies that prioritise rebuilding trust with stakeholders and strengthening the company's foundation.

Practical Guidance: Tips and Best Practices for Crisis Management

While every crisis is unique, the principles of good crisis management remain the same. Directors must focus on maintaining calm, assessing the situation clearly, and making decisions that protect the company's long-term viability. Below are key strategies and actionable advice for boards to consider during a crisis:

1. **Prepare with a Crisis Management Plan** A key part of crisis management is preparation. Boards should ensure that the company has a comprehensive crisis management plan in place, which should be reviewed and updated regularly. The plan should outline:

   - Potential crises and their implications
   - Roles and responsibilities for board members and senior executives
   - Clear communication protocols, both internally and externally
   - Steps for recovery and continuity planning

     - **Actionable Advice:** Boards should conduct regular crisis simulation exercises to test the effectiveness of the crisis management plan. These exercises help the board and management team identify potential gaps and improve response coordination.

2. **Maintain Transparent and Consistent Communication** In the midst of a crisis, communication is crucial. The board must ensure that communication with stakeholders—employees, customers, investors, and the public—is clear, transparent, and consistent. Misinformation or confusion can escalate a crisis and damage the company's reputation.

   - **Actionable Advice:** Establish a designated crisis communications team that can manage messaging across various platforms. Ensure that key messages are consistent across all communications and that updates are provided regularly.

3. **Empower the Management Team, But Maintain Oversight** While boards must provide strategic oversight during a crisis, directors should also trust and empower the management team to make operational decisions. The board's role is to guide,

monitor, and provide resources, while the management team handles the day-to-day response.

- o **Actionable Advice:** During a crisis, boards should avoid micromanaging. Instead, they should focus on ensuring the management team has the resources and authority they need to respond effectively. Board members should be available for strategic guidance but allow management to take the lead.

4. **Focus on Long-Term Recovery** Boards should avoid being solely reactive. They must balance the immediate response with long-term recovery and strategic adaptation. A successful crisis response not only resolves the immediate issue but also ensures that the company emerges stronger and more resilient.

- o **Actionable Advice:** Directors should engage in post-crisis reviews to evaluate the company's response, identify lessons learned, and implement measures to mitigate future risks. This can involve revisiting risk management frameworks, improving internal processes, or reinforcing corporate values.

5. **Maintain Stakeholder Trust** Trust is the foundation of any organisation's reputation. During a crisis, boards must work diligently to maintain the trust of employees, customers, investors, and other stakeholders. Upholding the company's values and demonstrating a commitment to ethical decision-making can help restore confidence.

- o **Actionable Advice:** Directors should actively engage with stakeholders, particularly customers and investors, to demonstrate that the company is handling the crisis with integrity. Transparency, empathy, and accountability should be at the forefront of these communications.

Table: Post-Crisis Evaluation Framework

Area	Evaluation Criteria	Next Steps
Communication	Clarity, transparency, and consistency	Implement a communication review process
Management Response	Speed, effectiveness, and alignment with strategy	Strengthen management protocols and training
Financial Impact	Direct and indirect costs of crisis response	Develop financial contingency plans
Reputation Recovery	Stakeholder trust and confidence post-crisis	Launch a reputation-building initiative

Interactive Element: Crisis Management Checklist

Crisis Management Readiness Checklist for Directors

1. **Crisis Plan & Protocols:**

   - Do we have a documented crisis management plan?
   - Is the plan regularly reviewed and updated?
   - Are all board members familiar with their roles in a crisis?

2. **Communication:**

   - Do we have a clear communication strategy for internal and external stakeholders?
   - Is there a designated spokesperson for the crisis?
   - Are crisis communications regularly updated?

3. **Management Empowerment:**

   - Does the management team have the authority to make decisions in a crisis?
   - Are the right resources available to the management team?
   - Is there a clear reporting line to the board during a crisis?

4. **Post-Crisis Recovery:**

   - Have we identified long-term recovery objectives?
   - Are we committed to addressing any issues that led to the crisis to prevent recurrence?
   - Are we working to restore stakeholder trust?

5. **Lessons Learned:**

   - Will we conduct a post-crisis review to identify lessons learned?
   - Are we integrating those lessons into future risk management and governance practices?

Discussion Question:

- How can boards balance the need for immediate action with the importance of making long-term, sustainable decisions during a crisis?

Key Takeaways & Summary

1. **Preparation is Key:** Boards must ensure that a comprehensive crisis management plan is in place, regularly tested, and updated. Proactive preparation is vital to handling crises effectively.
2. **Clear Communication Builds Trust:** Transparent and consistent communication with all stakeholders is essential to mitigate the impact of a crisis. The board must ensure that messaging is clear, honest, and empathetic.
3. **Empowerment and Oversight:** While directors must maintain oversight, they should trust the management team to execute the crisis response. Providing the right resources and guidance is essential to a successful resolution.
4. **Post-Crisis Recovery is Just as Important:** A crisis doesn't end when the immediate threat is over. Directors must focus on long-term recovery, learning from the crisis, and rebuilding trust among stakeholders.

By focusing on these principles, boards can ensure that they are not only capable of responding to crises but are also prepared to emerge stronger and more resilient in the aftermath.

Chapter 27

The Future of Corporate Governance

The Evolving Landscape of Corporate Governance

Corporate governance has always been an essential framework for guiding companies, ensuring accountability, transparency, and ethical behaviour. It encompasses the systems, processes, and principles through which companies are directed and controlled, with boards of directors playing a pivotal role in overseeing organisational strategy and performance. However, as the global business landscape evolves, so too must the practices and structures that underpin effective governance.

The next decade promises significant changes in corporate governance driven by multiple forces: technological advancements, shifting regulatory frameworks, societal demands, and changing stakeholder expectations. With the rise of AI, the expansion of Environmental, Social, and Governance (ESG) factors, and an increasingly globalised and interconnected business environment, directors will face new challenges and opportunities in their governance roles.

This chapter explores the trends shaping the future of corporate governance, offering insights into how boards can adapt to remain effective and relevant in an ever-changing world. We will look at emerging technologies like AI, evolving regulatory landscapes, and the growing importance of ESG considerations. By examining these trends, we aim to provide directors with the tools and strategies they need to prepare for the future of corporate governance.

Example: Walmart's Embrace of Digital Transformation

Walmart, one of the world's largest retail corporations, offers a compelling example of how governance can evolve to address technological disruption. In the early 2010s, Walmart faced mounting competition from e-commerce giants like Amazon, which were rapidly capturing market share by offering convenience, competitive pricing, and a seamless online shopping experience. Walmart's traditional business model, which relied heavily on physical stores, was at risk of becoming obsolete.

In response, Walmart's board of directors and leadership team embraced digital transformation, prioritising technology-driven innovation and adopting new strategies to remain competitive in the digital age.

Governance Actions and Strategic Pivot:

1. **Leadership Support for Digital Innovation:**

   Recognising the need for strong leadership in technology, Walmart's board supported the recruitment of tech-savvy executives, including Doug McMillon as CEO and Marc Lore, the founder of Jet.com, to lead Walmart's e-commerce operations. These appointments signalled Walmart's commitment to prioritising digital innovation.

2. **Acquisitions and Investments in Technology:**

   The board approved strategic acquisitions, such as the purchase of Jet.com in 2016, which brought advanced e-commerce capabilities and a younger, tech-driven culture into Walmart. Additionally, Walmart invested in its supply chain technology, warehouse automation, and artificial intelligence to improve efficiency and customer experience.

3. **Integration of Physical and Digital Operations:**

   Walmart's board endorsed the development of an omnichannel strategy, blending its vast network of physical stores with its online presence. Initiatives like online grocery pickup and Walmart+ (a subscription service competing with Amazon Prime) bridged the gap between in-store and online shopping.

4. **Continuous Risk Oversight:**

   The board established committees focused on technology and innovation, ensuring that digital transformation initiatives were aligned with Walmart's overall strategy and managed effectively. They also prioritised cybersecurity to safeguard customer data as the company's digital operations grew.

Outcomes and Lessons for Governance:

Walmart's ability to adapt its governance to prioritise technological transformation has proven successful. The company is now a leader in the omnichannel retail space, with a robust e-commerce platform that complements its physical stores. By 2023, Walmart's digital sales had grown exponentially, contributing significantly to its revenue.

Walmart's example highlights several critical lessons for boards:

- **Proactive Governance:** Boards must recognise disruptive trends early and support strategic pivots to address them.
- **Technology Expertise:** Having directors with expertise in technology and digital transformation is essential for navigating complex challenges.
- **Agility in Decision-Making:** Boards should be prepared to approve bold investments and innovative strategies, even when they disrupt traditional business models.

- **Integrated Approach:** Balancing physical assets with digital capabilities can create unique value propositions in industries undergoing technological disruption.

By aligning governance practices with the demands of technological change, Walmart demonstrated how boards could ensure long-term resilience and relevance in an evolving business landscape.

Trends Shaping the Future of Corporate Governance

1. Artificial Intelligence and Automation

The introduction of **AI** and automation technologies is perhaps the most disruptive trend reshaping corporate governance today. AI has the potential to revolutionise decision-making, streamline operations, and enhance strategic planning.

AI-powered analytics are already being used to monitor financial transactions in real-time, detect fraud, and analyse vast amounts of data to make better decisions. In corporate governance, AI can be leveraged to improve risk assessment, identify potential governance issues, and enhance overall board effectiveness.

However, with these advancements come significant challenges. The integration of AI into governance will require boards to understand the potential risks associated with these technologies, including biases in algorithmic decision-making and privacy concerns. Directors will need to be well-versed in these issues and ensure that AI technologies are implemented ethically and responsibly.

Expert Opinion: According to **Dr. Dambisa Moyo**, a renowned economist, "The future of corporate governance will be increasingly shaped by the technological revolution. Directors who are not well-versed in AI and data analytics will be at a disadvantage, as these technologies will shape not only business strategy but also governance processes."

2. Expanding Role of ESG (Environmental, Social, and Governance)

Another critical trend shaping the future of corporate governance is the increasing emphasis on **Environmental, Social, and Governance (ESG)** factors. ESG considerations have already gained traction among investors, regulators, and consumers, with companies being held accountable not only for their financial performance but also for their impact on society and the environment.

The future of governance will see ESG issues taking centre stage in boardrooms. Corporate boards will need to develop expertise in these areas and integrate them into their decision-making frameworks. This includes monitoring the environmental footprint of operations, ensuring diversity and inclusion at all levels, and promoting ethical business practices.

Governance structures will increasingly incorporate **sustainable practices**, ensuring that companies create long-term value for all stakeholders, including shareholders, employees, and the wider community. As pressure increases from both stakeholders and regulators, boards must proactively address ESG concerns rather than responding reactively.

Real-World Example: A company leading the charge in ESG integration is **Unilever**. As part of its commitment to sustainability, Unilever has committed to achieving **net-zero emissions by 2039** and has been actively working to embed sustainability throughout its supply chain and product portfolio. Unilever's governance model reflects the growing importance of ESG, with the board taking an active role in overseeing the company's sustainability initiatives. This forward-thinking governance approach has enhanced the company's reputation and attracted investors focused on long-term sustainable growth.

3. Evolving Regulatory Landscape

The regulatory environment surrounding corporate governance is constantly evolving, and future governance will need to be responsive to these changes. As global financial markets become more interconnected, regulators are placing increasing emphasis on transparency, accountability, and ethical practices.

The introduction of **new regulations** related to ESG disclosures, cybersecurity, and corporate responsibility will require boards to stay informed and adapt their governance practices accordingly. **Data privacy laws**, such as the **General Data Protection Regulation (GDPR)** in the European Union, are a prime example of how regulations are changing to protect consumer rights and address the ethical use of data. Corporate boards will need to ensure compliance with these regulations and create robust systems for managing risks associated with data privacy and security.

Moreover, with increasing regulatory scrutiny on executive compensation and corporate tax practices, directors will need to ensure that their organisations adhere to best practices and comply with new standards.

Expert Opinion: Dr. Robert G. Eccles, a professor at Harvard Business School, suggests that "The increasing global focus on regulation will lead to more standardised governance practices, but at the same time, companies will be expected to adopt governance models that are adaptable to local contexts and stakeholders."

4. The Growing Role of Stakeholders and Activist Investors

Another significant trend shaping corporate governance is the **growing influence of stakeholders and activist investors**. In the past, governance was primarily concerned with serving the interests of shareholders. However, as the definition of corporate responsibility has expanded, boards are now expected to consider a broader range of stakeholders, including employees, customers, suppliers, and the communities in which the company operates.

Activist investors are increasingly vocal in their demands for changes in corporate governance. These investors are using their shareholder power to push for changes in executive compensation, corporate strategy, and even governance structures. Boards must engage with these investors and ensure that they have a clear understanding of their company's long-term strategy and governance practices.

This shift will require directors to be more transparent in their decision-making processes and to ensure that they are acting in the best interests of all stakeholders, not just shareholders.

Practical Advice for Directors in Preparing for the Future of Governance

1. **Stay Informed About Technology and AI:**

    As AI and automation become more prevalent, directors should educate themselves on the latest technological advancements and their potential impact on governance. This includes understanding how AI can improve decision-making and how to mitigate associated risks.

2. **Integrate ESG into the Core Business Strategy:**

    ESG is not just a compliance issue but a strategic opportunity. Directors should ensure that ESG goals are integrated into the company's long-term business strategy and that the board is actively engaged in overseeing ESG initiatives.

3. **Strengthen Cybersecurity and Data Privacy Oversight:**

    As cyber threats continue to grow, boards must prioritise cybersecurity and data privacy. This includes establishing clear governance frameworks for managing cybersecurity risks and ensuring that the company complies with data protection regulations.

4. **Engage with Stakeholders and Activist Investors:**

   Directors should engage in proactive communication with stakeholders and activist investors, ensuring that their governance practices align with the expectations of a broad range of stakeholders.

5. **Be Prepared for Regulatory Changes:**

   Given the rapidly evolving regulatory environment, boards should stay informed about changes in laws and regulations, particularly those related to ESG, data privacy, and corporate responsibility.

Interactive Element: Discussion Questions for Directors

1. How can AI and automation be incorporated into our governance practices to improve decision-making?
2. What steps can we take to strengthen our company's ESG strategy and ensure long-term sustainability?
3. How can we enhance stakeholder engagement and ensure that we are considering the interests of all stakeholders in our decision-making?
4. What steps should we take to ensure that we are compliant with evolving regulatory requirements?
5. How can we prepare for potential activist investors and ensure that our governance practices are transparent and aligned with stakeholder expectations?

Key Takeaways

1. The future of corporate governance will be shaped by emerging technologies, evolving regulatory frameworks, and growing societal expectations around ESG.

2. Directors must be proactive in integrating AI, ESG, and cybersecurity into their governance practices to ensure that their organisations remain resilient and adaptable.
3. Ongoing education, stakeholder engagement, and transparent decision-making will be critical for boards in the coming years.
4. Corporate governance is no longer just about financial performance; it is about creating long-term value for all stakeholders, ensuring that businesses act responsibly, sustainably, and ethically in an increasingly complex world.

This chapter serves as a roadmap for directors navigating the rapidly changing landscape of corporate governance. By embracing new technologies, adapting to regulatory shifts, and addressing stakeholder demands, boards can secure a prosperous and sustainable future for their organisations.

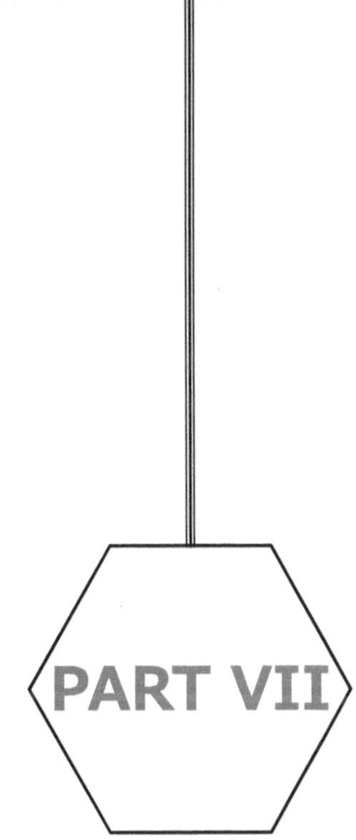

Boards in Action: From Vision to Reality

Chapter 28

Real-World Insights: Board of Directors in Action

Global Governance Practices

Board governance is pivotal to the strategic direction, sustainability, and ethical standards of a company. By examining real-world case studies from a range of regions and industries, including the UAE, we can gain valuable insights into effective governance practices and the impact of boards on organisational outcomes. This section presents a series of mini-case studies, each highlighting the significant contributions or failures of boards and directors, with lessons drawn from these experiences to benefit current and future board members.

1. Global Governance Practices

Comparing Board Structures and Practices in Different Regions

1. NORTH AMERICA (U.S. AND CANADA)

Governance Overview:

- North America's governance systems typically feature a mix of executive and non-executive directors, with a growing emphasis on **independent directors** to avoid conflicts of interest.
- Regulatory frameworks like the **Sarbanes-Oxley Act** (2002) have shaped governance practices to emphasise transparency and accountability.

Key Example: Walmart's Governance Evolution Walmart transitioned to a more independent board structure with robust governance practices, prioritising ethics, diversity, and sustainability to align with the company's global scale.

2. EUROPE (UK AND EU)

Governance Overview:

- The UK and EU prioritise **shareholder value** and **sustainability** in their governance practices. A notable example is the separation of the roles of CEO and Chairman to ensure board independence.

Key Example: Unilever's Dual-Board Model Unilever employs a two-tier board structure, blending governance and executive functions, with a focus on long-term sustainability, making it a global leader in responsible business practices.

3. ASIA (CHINA, JAPAN, AND INDIA)

Governance Overview:

- Asia has a more complex relationship between government, family ownership, and corporate governance, particularly in China and Japan.
- In India, **CSR** (Corporate Social Responsibility) is increasingly integrated into governance frameworks, especially in large conglomerates.

Key Example: Tata Group in India Tata's focus on ethical governance, sustainability, and transparency sets a high standard for corporate boards in India, fostering trust in one of the nation's largest conglomerates.

4. THE UAE'S UNIQUE GOVERNANCE STRUCTURE

Governance Overview:

- The UAE's corporate governance landscape is influenced by its position as a global business hub. It is heavily shaped by local regulations and by the presence of family-owned businesses, which are common in the region.

- Governance structures are being modernised, with the introduction of laws like the **UAE Corporate Governance Code** to standardise practices across sectors.

Key Example: DP World's Governance Transformation DP World, a global leader in logistics and ports, has undergone significant changes in its governance structure to ensure board independence, transparency, and adherence to global governance standards while maintaining its family ties.

Best Practices from Global Leaders in Governance

- **Board Diversity**: Companies like **Goldman Sachs** and **Citigroup** prioritise diversity in their board compositions, focusing on various backgrounds and skills to enhance decision-making.
- **Risk Management**: Global companies like **HSBC** have demonstrated a strong focus on governance with rigorous risk management frameworks.
- **Sustainability**: Companies such as **Patagonia** exemplify the integration of environmental responsibility into corporate governance, driven by a commitment to ethical practices.

Director Case Studies

Introduction

In this section, we explore influential directors whose leadership and strategic vision shaped the future of their respective organisations. These directors represent a range of industries, including global leaders in sustainability, innovation, and financial governance.

1. Indra Nooyi at PepsiCo (Global)

Impact on Governance:

- As the Chairwoman and CEO of PepsiCo, Nooyi implemented the **Performance with Purpose** strategy, balancing business success with social responsibility.

- Her efforts transformed PepsiCo's approach to health-conscious products, diversity, and sustainability.

Key Lessons for Directors:

- Directors must ensure a holistic view that combines business growth with sustainability and social impact.
- Leadership in governance requires both strategic thinking and responsibility to the broader community.

2. Warren Buffett at Berkshire Hathaway (Global)

Impact on Governance:

- Buffett's philosophy of decentralisation and trust in management shaped the structure of Berkshire Hathaway's board.
- He famously advocated for "trusting managers to run their businesses" while keeping the board's focus on ethics and transparency.

Key Lessons for Directors:

- A board must establish clear ethical guidelines but also empower management to execute the strategy with minimal interference.

3. Sheryl Sandberg at Facebook (Global)

Impact on Governance:

- As COO of Facebook, Sandberg helped expand the company's advertising model. However, she faced significant scrutiny over the platform's role in misinformation and privacy concerns.
- Her approach to growth, although successful financially, sparked questions about ethical decision-making.

Key Lessons for Directors:

- Boards must ensure growth strategies are aligned with ethical considerations and social responsibility.

- Ethical decision-making is central to maintaining a company's long-term reputation.

4. Sheikh Ahmed bin Saeed Al Maktoum at Emirates Airline (UAE)

Impact on Governance:

- As Chairman and CEO of Emirates, Sheikh Ahmed's governance has been critical in transforming Emirates into a world-leading airline.
- His focus on innovation, leadership, and strategic alliances (such as with **Qantas**) has made Emirates a globally recognised brand.

Key Lessons for Directors:

- A board should support visionary leadership and foster long-term partnerships that align with the company's goals.
- Directors must understand the role of government and strategic alliances in a competitive industry like aviation.

5. Emaar Properties' Board Leadership (UAE)

Impact on Governance:

- Emaar's growth into one of the UAE's largest real estate developers is directly attributed to its board's strategic foresight under the leadership of Chairman Mohamed Alabbar.
- The company's board was instrumental in creating landmark developments, including **Burj Khalifa**, by focusing on vision, risk management, and long-term investment.

Key Lessons for Directors:

- Directors must maintain a clear vision for the future, understanding that large-scale projects require long-term strategies and risk management.
- Boards should drive innovation and not shy away from ambitious projects that align with national growth strategies.

Lessons from Board Failures

In contrast to successful boards, there are numerous examples where governance failures led to dramatic consequences. This section delves into some of the most significant board failures and examines the red flags that were ignored, the poor decision-making processes, and the lessons to be learned.

1. Wirecard Scandal (Germany)

What Went Wrong:

Wirecard, once a high-flying fintech company in Germany, collapsed in 2020 due to a massive accounting fraud that involved the company overstating its financial position by €1.9 billion.

- The company's board, including CEO Markus Braun and CFO Jan Marsalek, engaged in fraudulent activities, creating false financial reports to deceive investors and regulators.
- Despite multiple warning signs from whistleblowers, the board failed to exercise independent oversight, allowing the scandal to grow undetected for years.
- Wirecard's board also failed to ensure that its audit processes were robust enough to detect fraudulent financial statements, allowing the company to remain publicly traded even as the fraud escalated.

Key Lessons for Directors:

- **Independent Oversight**: A truly independent audit and risk committee can be a crucial line of defence against fraudulent activities.
- **Scrutiny of Financial Reporting**: Boards must maintain an unwavering focus on the integrity of financial reports and ensure transparency, especially in complex industries like fintech.
- **Acting on Red Flags**: Directors should act quickly when fraud or irregularities are suspected, regardless of the company's reputation or its potential for growth.

2. Carillion's Insolvency (UK)

What Went Wrong:

Carillion, a UK-based construction and facilities management company, went into liquidation in 2018 after failing to meet its financial obligations, resulting in the loss of thousands of jobs and millions in pension liabilities.

- The board overestimated the company's ability to meet its obligations and failed to manage cash flow, leading to a severe liquidity crisis.
- The board ignored multiple warning signs, including large losses on major projects, escalating debts, and unpaid bills, while maintaining a positive public image of financial health.
- Despite the company's growing debt, the board continued to make risky business decisions, including bidding for large government contracts without assessing the financial risks involved.

Key Lessons for Directors:

- **Financial Prudence and Risk Management:** Boards must prioritise financial prudence and ensure that the company is not over-leveraged or reliant on unsustainable growth.
- **Honest Assessment of Risks:** Directors should challenge overly optimistic assumptions about the business and assess risks honestly, especially when undertaking major projects or seeking external funding.
- **Liquidity and Cash Flow Management:** A solid understanding of cash flow and liquidity is essential for boards to make informed decisions, particularly when dealing with large contracts or volatile markets.

3. Abraaj Group's Collapse (UAE)

What Went Wrong:

Abraaj Group, once a prominent private equity firm in the Middle East, faced a dramatic collapse in 2018 due to its alleged financial mismanagement, misuse of investor funds, and lack of effective oversight by its board.

- The company, led by founder Arif Naqvi, expanded aggressively across emerging markets, particularly in healthcare, but ran into liquidity issues after overstating its financial performance.
- The board failed to act decisively when whistleblower reports about financial discrepancies surfaced, and did not ensure adequate checks and balances on the company's practices.
- Abraaj was also heavily reliant on external financing, making it vulnerable when investors pulled back, leading to its eventual insolvency.

Key Lessons for Directors:

- **Independent Oversight**: Boards must ensure that financial practices are transparent and that there is a strong, independent audit function. They must act on red flags raised by whistleblowers or other stakeholders.
- **Financial Prudence**: A sound financial structure, free from over-leverage, is critical to avoiding crises.
- **Timely Intervention**: Directors must be proactive and intervene early when there are concerns about financial performance or the integrity of the company's operations.

4. Toshiba Accounting Scandal (Japan)

What Went Wrong:

Toshiba, one of Japan's largest conglomerates, was embroiled in a major accounting scandal that came to light in 2015. Over a period of several years, the company overstated its profits by more than $1.2 billion.

- Toshiba's board failed to uncover the fraudulent accounting practices carried out by senior executives who had been inflating profits to meet aggressive earnings targets.

- The board's lack of independence and failure to act on internal whistleblower reports allowed the issue to persist for years, eroding shareholder trust and damaging the company's reputation.
- Senior executives manipulated financial results to avoid missing targets, creating a false image of financial health, which ultimately led to significant financial restatements and a decline in shareholder value.

Key Lessons for Directors:

- **Importance of Ethical Leadership and Board Independence:** Boards should ensure that company leadership upholds the highest standards of ethics and that there is a robust system of independent oversight.
- **Rigorous Financial Oversight:** Directors must ensure that financial reporting is closely monitored, with strong internal controls and regular external audits to detect and prevent any discrepancies or fraudulent activity.
- **Promote a Culture of Transparency:** It's essential for boards to foster an organisational culture that prioritises transparency and openness, encouraging employees and executives to report concerns without fear of retaliation.

The diverse range of case studies explored—spanning global governance practices, leadership impacts, and board failures—provides valuable lessons for directors today. The ability to make informed, ethical, and strategic decisions is critical to the success of both individual organisations and the broader corporate landscape. Directors must recognise the importance of transparency, independence, and foresight, continually striving.

Chapter 29

The Game-Changer – The Power of an Active, Visionary Board

As the sun sets on this journey through the world of boards of directors, we find ourselves at a pivotal moment—one where the lessons learned, the challenges faced, and the principles outlined all converge. This is not just the end of a book; it's the beginning of a transformation. For too long, boards have been viewed as ceremonial, passive entities, reduced to a checklist of names on paper. But as we've explored throughout these pages, the true power of a board lies in its ability to lead, challenge, innovate, and steer the organisation toward lasting success. In this final chapter, we will take the core lessons we've learned and bring them into focus, offering a vision for the future where boards aren't just a formality but an active, strategic partner driving change and growth. This is your call to action—to embrace the immense potential of a dynamic, empowered board and to lead your organisation into a new era of leadership and possibility.

Beyond the Boardroom: Key Pillars for Transformative Governance

As we conclude, let us reflect on the essence of what defines a truly empowered and effective board. This book is not about abstract theories or lofty ideals; it is a guide shaped by hard-earned lessons and practical insights that boards of all sizes can implement to achieve meaningful impact.

An exceptional board is one that transcends routine governance, becoming a dynamic force that shapes the future of its organisation.

To inspire you on this path, here are some key principles to carry forward:

1. **Diversity Fuels Excellence**

   True diversity extends beyond surface-level traits. Boards thrive when they embrace varied perspectives, experiences, and expertise, fostering innovation and resilience.

2. **Governance Builds Trust**

   Ethical leadership, transparency, and accountability form the foundation of effective governance. A board that champions these values earns the confidence of stakeholders and steers the organisation toward sustainable success.

3. **Strategic Leadership**

   Boards are not mere spectators but active architects of strategy. By challenging assumptions, championing long-term goals, and driving innovation, they become catalysts for growth.

4. **Adaptability Is Non-Negotiable**

   In an ever-changing world, agility is key. Forward-looking boards anticipate disruptions, embrace technological advancements, and pivot swiftly to seize opportunities.

5. **Succession Secures Continuity**

   Leadership transitions are inevitable. A proactive approach to succession planning ensures stability and positions the organisation for sustained performance.

6. **Balance Oversight and Empowerment**

   The most effective boards strike a balance between providing robust oversight and empowering management to execute with creativity and autonomy.

7. **Clear Communication is Power**

> Open, honest and transparent communication fosters trust and collaboration. A board united in purpose and clarity is better positioned to lead decisively.

This journey is not about merely avoiding pitfalls; it is about embracing the full potential of boardroom leadership. A high-performing board is not just a governing body – it is a strategic partner, a visionary collective, and a beacon of accountability and innovation.

The path to boardroom excellence is ongoing, requiring constant reflection, adaptation, and dedication. But the rewards—organisational growth, societal impact, and enduring legacy—are immeasurable.

Dispelling Myths: Boards Are Not Just Formalities

One of the most persistent myths we must confront is the idea that boards are mere formalities – a box to check for legal compliance. Unfortunately, too many organisations see their boards as little more than a group of names on a letterhead, called into action only when a major decision needs to be approved. This couldn't be further from the truth.

Think of the board as the co-pilot in a high-performance jet. The CEO is in the cockpit, but the board is there to help navigate the skies. They aren't there to simply observe the smooth flights, but to prepare for the turbulence ahead. They're in the game—not on the sidelines.

A well-functioning board isn't just a rubber stamp committee. It is an essential strategic partner. It challenges assumptions, provides foresight, and ensures that the company is equipped to handle both opportunities and obstacles. It has the power to catalyse innovation and drive the business forward.

The Future of Boards: A Vision of Empowered Leadership

Now, imagine a future where every organisation, no matter the size or industry, sees its board as a strategic asset. Picture a company where the board is fully engaged—not just in overseeing operations but in actively shaping the direction of the business, fostering a culture of accountability and innovation.

Boards in this future will be more than compliance checklists. They will be champions of growth and change. They will work hand in hand with management, offering insights, fresh perspectives, and guidance. They will not only keep an eye on risks but actively seek out opportunities for transformation and reinvention. They will hold the company to its highest standards of integrity, ensuring that long-term success is achieved in a sustainable and responsible way.

For business owners, entrepreneurs, and CEOs, this vision should excite you. The board you build can and should be a source of strength, not just a group to approve decisions. It should be a sounding board, a guiding hand, and a trusted adviser. If you're not leveraging the full potential of your board, now is the time to rethink it.

For current board members, this is your call to action. Don't just show up for meetings. Don't just sign off on the CEO's plans. Engage. Challenge. Innovate. This is your moment to step into your full potential and help shape the future of the organisation.

A Call to Action: Building the Board You Need

As we wrap up this journey, I challenge you to reflect:

- **Is your board a strategic asset or just a formality?**
- **Are your board members equipped to meet the challenges of today's rapidly changing landscape?**
- **Are you actively working to ensure your board is diverse, dynamic, and ready to tackle the big issues?**

This is your time to act. Whether you're a startup founder, the CEO of an established company, or a business owner looking to grow, you have the power to shape your board into a force for good. Take the principles discussed in this book and use them to assess, revamp, and empower your board. Whether you're building a board from scratch or revitalising an existing one, your approach matters.

The road to a high-functioning board is not without its challenges, but the rewards are worth it. You'll have a team that's ready to tackle complex problems, seize new opportunities, and navigate the toughest of situations. Your board will be a cornerstone of your company's success.

Don't wait until the next crisis. Start now. Empower your board. Build a team that's not just there to watch from the sidelines, but to lead with you, alongside you, in the exciting journey ahead.

The future is calling. Will your board be ready?

Chapter 30

Pathways to the Boardroom – How You Can Get There

As we conclude this exploration of corporate governance dynamics, it's time to focus on practical steps for stepping into a board of directors role. Whether you are an aspiring board member, a seasoned professional seeking to transition, or someone aiming to enhance your influence, this chapter provides valuable guidance on making that leap.

The future of boards is changing, and the path to becoming a board member is evolving too. It's no longer about simply having a certain title or position; modern boards demand diverse skills, strategic thinking, and leadership capabilities. Below, I will detail **10 different ways** you can enter the boardroom, the educational qualifications required, and how to align with the evolving composition of the modern board.

1. Develop a Strong Track Record in Leadership Roles

How to Enter:

Start by excelling in senior leadership roles within your organisation, whether as a **CXO, entrepreneur, or department head**. Demonstrating leadership skills, driving results, and having a proven ability to solve complex business challenges positions you as an attractive candidate for board membership.

Advice:

The modern board looks for individuals who have managed large teams, handled high-level strategic decisions, and driven business transformation. Your leadership journey should reflect your ability to make strategic decisions, mitigate risks, and steer an organisation towards growth.

2. Build Expertise in Key Business Areas

How to Enter:

Focus on gaining expertise in areas like **finance, marketing, operations, technology, or risk management**. Specialising in one of these key business areas makes you an attractive board candidate, particularly if the company is facing challenges in these domains.

Advice:

For example, if you're a **CFO**, your deep understanding of finance and governance will be invaluable for audit committees. Similarly, a **technology executive** with expertise in innovation and digital transformation can serve on boards looking to navigate tech disruptions.

3. Strengthen Your Financial and Governance Knowledge

How to Enter:

Pursue qualifications like **Chartered Accountant (CA), CPA, CFA, or MBA,** with a focus on corporate governance, business strategy, and legal frameworks. Developing a solid understanding of corporate finance, financial reporting, risk management, and governance principles is essential for board members to navigate the complexities of modern organisations effectively.

Advice:

Modern boards are increasingly focused on governance, compliance, and legal oversight, making financial literacy and legal acumen critical skills. Adding advanced qualifications in law, business analytics, or executive education programmes specialising in board governance will further enhance your credibility and readiness for board roles.

4. Engage in Mentorship and Board Advisory Roles

How to Enter:

Serve in an advisory capacity for businesses, startups, or non-profits. Often, these roles lead to board invitations, as you will have demonstrated your capacity to advise and guide leadership teams on strategic and financial matters.

Advice:

Being involved in mentorship programmes, advisory boards, or committees provides practical exposure to governance issues and helps you build a network of influential leaders. This experience is a stepping stone to full board membership.

5. Get Involved with Non-Profit or Charitable Boards

How to Enter:

Start by serving on the board of a **non-profit organisation.** Non-profits often have a less formal selection process, and these roles can offer hands-on experience in governance. Over time, this exposure helps you gain experience and the credentials needed to transition to for-profit boards.

Advice:

Non-profit boards are excellent training grounds for governance. You will learn how to balance financial performance with social impact, manage stakeholder expectations, and lead diverse teams, all valuable skills for future board roles.

6. Tap Into Your Network

How to Enter:

Leverage your network to gain introductions to board members or recruiters specialising in board placements. Attend board governance conferences, seminars, and workshops to meet decision-makers and learn about board vacancies.

Advice:

Networking is critical in gaining access to board positions. Build relationships with senior executives, headhunters, and other board members who can guide you or recommend you for positions. Stay active in industry groups or professional organisations where board members meet.

7. Gain Experience Through Executive Education and Specialised Programmes

How to Enter:

Enrol in executive education programmes focused on **corporate governance**, such as the **Harvard Business School's Board Governance Programme** or the **INSEAD Directors' Programme**. These programmes provide valuable insights into board dynamics and allow you to connect with like-minded professionals.

Advice:

These specialised programmes enhance your understanding of the boardroom, teach you about regulatory requirements, and expose you to the intricacies of board decision-making. Graduating from such programmes signals to boards that you are prepared for leadership at the highest level.

8. Focus on Diversity and Inclusion Expertise

How to Enter:

As diversity becomes a key focus in modern boards, specialise in **diversity and inclusion (D&I)**. Companies are actively looking for directors who understand the importance of diverse perspectives and the role they play in driving innovation and growth.

Advice:

If you have a passion for D&I, equip yourself with the knowledge and skills to guide organisations through their diversity journey. This could be your unique angle for securing a board seat, particularly for organisations prioritising diverse leadership.

9. Leverage International Experience

How to Enter:

If you have international business experience, particularly in emerging markets, your global perspective is highly valued by boards looking to expand internationally or manage cross-border operations.

Advice:

International experience brings a broader perspective, strategic vision, and understanding of global markets. With companies expanding globally, boards value members who can offer insights into diverse cultures, regulatory environments, and market dynamics.

10. Position Yourself as a Thought Leader

How to Enter:

Write articles, give talks, or engage in thought leadership within your industry. Share your expertise on governance, strategy, innovation, or leadership through blogs, webinars, or industry panels. Being recognised as an expert will attract board invitations.

Advice:

When you position yourself as a thought leader, your reputation grows within the industry. Thought leadership demonstrates to boards that you have the knowledge, foresight, and communication skills to make a significant impact.

The Composition of the Modern Board

As you prepare to step into the boardroom, it's important to understand that the **composition of modern boards** is rapidly evolving. Boards today are more diverse, more strategic, and more forward-thinking. The following are key characteristics of today's board composition:

- **Diversity of Thought**: Modern boards look for directors who bring different perspectives and skill sets, whether from various industries, cultural backgrounds, or professional disciplines.
- **Technology Expertise**: With digital transformation taking centre stage, boards are increasingly prioritising technology-savvy directors who can guide the organisation through technological disruptions.
- **Sustainability and ESG Focus**: Boards are also placing emphasis on environmental, social, and governance (ESG) expertise, with directors who can navigate sustainability challenges and create long-term value for shareholders and society.
- **Independence**: Independence remains a cornerstone of modern boards, with the need for independent directors who can provide unbiased oversight and challenge management when necessary.
- **Continuous Learning**: The most effective boards are those that engage in ongoing education and self-assessment to remain relevant in a fast-changing business landscape.

Final Advice for Aspiring Board Members

As you look to step into the boardroom, remember that being a director is not just about overseeing a company; it's about adding strategic value, fostering innovation, and making decisions that impact the organisation's future. Cultivate your skills, build relationships, and stay true to your purpose as a leader. The boardroom is calling—make sure you're ready to answer.

Appendix

Governance Documents for Effective Board Operations

1. Board Charter: A Foundational Document for Effective Governance

Purpose

The Board Charter outlines the purpose, authority, and responsibilities of the board of directors, establishing the framework for governance practices and operational effectiveness. It serves as a guiding document to ensure accountability, transparency, and alignment with organisational goals.

Key Components

1. **Board Composition and Qualifications**

   - Defines the required expertise, experience, and diversity of board members.
   - Includes provisions for independent directors to ensure objective decision-making.

2. **Roles and Responsibilities**

   - **Board Members:** Oversight of strategy, risk management and performance monitoring.
   - **Committees:** Clear mandates for specialised committees such as Audit, Compensation, and Governance.

3. **Meeting Frequency and Decision-Making Authority.**

   - Sets a schedule for regular and special meetings (e.g. quarterly or ad hoc).

- ○ Details quorum requirements and decision-making processes, including voting rights.

4. **Governance Practices**

   - ○ Articulates the board's commitment to ethical leadership and compliance with governance codes.
   - ○ Ensures the clear separation of roles between the board and executive management to avoid conflicts.

Real-World Example

A publicly traded tech company specialises in its Board Charter:

- A minimum of two independent directors to maintain impartiality.
- Quarterly board meetings dedicated to evaluating financial results and approving strategic initiatives.
- An annual review of risk assessments and executive performance.

Best Practices for Implementation

- **Legal Alignment:** Ensure compliance with jurisdictional governance codes and legal requirements, such as UAE Corporate Governance Regulations or international standards like the OECD Principles.
- **Clarity and Precision:** Clearly define roles, avoiding overlaps between board and management responsibilities.
- **Periodic Updates:** Review the charter annually to reflect changes in corporate strategy, regulatory updates, or board composition.
- **Stakeholder Transparency:** Make the charter accessible to shareholders to build trust and demonstrate commitment to robust governance.

2. Code of Conduct: Upholding Ethics and Integrity

Purpose

The Code of Conduct establishes the ethical framework for directors and management, promoting trust, integrity, and accountability. It guides decision-making and behaviour, ensuring alignment with the organisation's values and legal requirements.

Key Components

1. **Confidentiality and Data Security.**

   - Protect sensitive company information and maintain confidentiality at all times.
   - Prohibit unauthorised disclosure of proprietary data or trade secrets.

2. **Conflicts of Interest**

   - Require full disclosure of potential conflicts to avoid compromised decision-making.
   - Outline steps to manage or recuse from decisions involving personal interests.

3. **Compliance with Laws and Regulations**

   - Ensure adherence to applicable legal frameworks, governance codes, and industry standards.
   - Address issues such as bribery, corruption, and fair competition.

4. **Insider Trading and Whistleblower Protection**

   - Prohibit trading in material non-public information and provide clear guidelines for reporting insider violations.
   - Establish a secure mechanism for whistleblowers to report unethical behaviour without fear of retaliation.

Hypothetical Scenario

Before a major acquisition vote, a director discloses a personal financial interest in the target company. Following the Code of Conduct, the director recuses themselves from discussions and decisions, ensuring an impartial process and maintaining the board's integrity.

Best Practices for Implementation

- **Illustrate Ethical Dilemmas:** Include real-world or hypothetical scenarios to provide practical guidance.
- **Regular Training:** Conduct periodic training sessions for directors and management to reinforce ethical standards and clarify expectations.
- **Compliance Monitoring:** Establish mechanisms for monitoring adherence to the code, such as audits or compliance reviews.
- **Accountability Measures:** Define consequences for violations to ensure the code is respected and enforced consistently.

3. Board Meeting Agenda Template: Structuring Effective Meetings

Purpose

The Board Meeting Agenda provides a structured framework to streamline discussions, allocate time effectively, and ensure all critical issues are addressed. It promotes focused decision-making and enhances board productivity.

Key Components

1. **Opening Formalities**

   - **Call to Order:** The chairperson initiates the meeting.
   - **Quorum Check:** Confirm attendance to meet decision-making requirements.
   - **Approval of Previous Minutes:** Review and endorse minutes from the last meeting.

2. **Strategic Discussions**

   - Address key priorities such as organisational strategy, risk management, and market opportunities.
   - Allocate ample time to discuss high-impact items.

3. **Routine Business.**

   - Review operational updates, financial performance, and compliance matters.
   - Cover administrative issues, such as approving policies or budgets.

4. **Committee Reports**

   - Present findings and recommendations from subcommittees (e.g. Audit, Compensation, Risk).
   - Allow for questions and clarifications on committee outcomes.

5. **Action Items and Follow-ups**

   - Summarise key takeaways and assign responsibilities for unresolved items.
   - Establish deadlines for follow-up actions.

6. **Closing Formalities**

   - Address deferred items in the "Parking Lot" section.
   - Confirm the date and agenda for the next meeting.
   - Adjournment.

Hypothetical Scenario

During a period of economic volatility, the agenda prioritises a 45-minute discussion on risk management strategies, including contingency planning and market analysis. This focus helps the board mitigate potential threats and make proactive decisions.

Best Practices for Implementation

- **Advance Distribution:** Share the agenda and supporting materials at least one week before the meeting to allow thorough preparation.
- **Time Allocation:** Assign specific time slots for each item to ensure comprehensive discussions without overextending the meeting.
- **Flexibility:** Include a "Parking Lot" section to revisit deferred items or issues arising during the meeting.
- **Feedback Loop:** Collect input from board members on agenda effectiveness to refine future iterations.

4. Board Meeting Minutes Template

Purpose

Board Meeting Minutes serve as an official record of decisions, discussions, and attendance. They ensure accountability, provide a historical reference, and fulfil legal and regulatory requirements.

Key Components

1. **Header Information**

   - Meeting date, time, location, and mode (e.g., in-person, virtual).
   - Names of attendees, absentees, and guests.

2. **Approval of Previous Minutes**

   - Reference to the prior meeting's minutes and confirmation of approval or amendments.

3. **Agenda Items and Discussions**

   - Summaries of discussions, focusing on key points without divulging sensitive details.
   - Action items assigned, with responsible parties and deadlines.

4. **Motions and Voting Outcomes**

   - Documentation of motions raised, seconded, and the results of votes (e.g., approved, denied, or deferred).
   - Include the names of directors who voted against or abstained, if applicable.

5. **Reports and Presentations**

   - Highlights from committee reports, management updates, or external presentations.

6. **Closing and Next Steps**

   - Recap of unresolved items, next meeting schedule, and adjournment time.

Legal Considerations

- **Evidence in Legal Disputes:** Meeting minutes may be scrutinised during regulatory reviews or lawsuits, making accuracy critical.
- **Compliance:** Ensure the minutes comply with laws governing corporate governance (e.g., UAE Commercial Companies Law, Sarbanes-Oxley Act).
- **Confidentiality:** Avoid including information that may compromise the organisation's competitive or legal standing.

Best Practices for Implementation

- **Dedicated Minute-Taker:** Assign a professional familiar with governance language to ensure precise recording.
- **Standardised Format:** Use a consistent template to enhance clarity and ease of reference.
- **Timely Approval:** Distribute draft minutes promptly after the meeting for review and approval in the next session.
- **Archiving:** Maintain organised records that are easily accessible for audits or board reference.

5. Risk Assessment Matrix Template

Purpose

A Risk Assessment Matrix enables boards to systematically identify, evaluate, and prioritise risks based on their likelihood and impact. It supports informed decision-making and helps allocate resources effectively to mitigate potential threats.

Key Components

1. **Risk Categories**

   - **Strategic Risks:** Market changes, competition, or disruptions to business models.
   - **Operational Risks:** Supply chain issues, IT failures, or process inefficiencies.
   - **Financial Risks:** Liquidity challenges, currency fluctuations, or fraud.
   - **Compliance Risks:** Regulatory breaches or legal disputes.

2. **Matrix Columns**

   - **Risk Description:** Concise summary of each identified risk.
   - **Likelihood:** Probability of the risk occurring (e.g., high, medium, low).
   - **Impact:** Severity of consequences if the risk materialises (e.g., critical, moderate, minor).
   - **Mitigation Measures:** Strategies and actions to reduce or manage the risk.
   - **Responsible Parties:** Individuals or teams tasked with managing specific risks.

3. **Prioritisation Framework**

   - Use a scoring system (e.g., 1–5 scale) for likelihood and impact to create a visual heatmap of risks.

Real-World Example

A global manufacturing firm uses a Risk Assessment Matrix to address supply chain vulnerabilities during a pandemic. Risks such as supplier delays and transportation bottlenecks are rated as high-impact and high-likelihood, prompting the board to diversify suppliers and invest in regional warehouses.

Best Practices for Implementation

- **Regular Updates:** Review and revise the matrix quarterly or as new risks emerge, such as geopolitical tensions or technological advancements.
- **Integration:** Embed the matrix into the company's Enterprise Risk Management (ERM) framework to ensure alignment with overall risk strategies.
- **Cross-Functional Input:** Involve various departments (e.g., finance, operations, IT) to capture a comprehensive view of risks.
- **Clear Reporting:** Use visuals like heatmaps or dashboards to communicate risks effectively to the board and stakeholders.
- **Focus on Mitigation:** Prioritise actionable mitigation measures and allocate resources to address the most critical risks.

6. Succession Planning Template: Securing Leadership Continuity

Purpose

A Succession Planning Template ensures smooth transitions in board or executive leadership by identifying and preparing potential successors for key roles. It mitigates risks associated with leadership changes and supports organisational stability.

Key Components

1. **Key Role Identification**

    o   Define critical board and executive positions vital to achieving strategic goals.
    o   Outline role responsibilities, competencies, and success criteria.

2. **Potential Successor Identification**

    o   List internal and external candidates with the skills and potential to fill key roles.
    o   Categorise candidates as "ready now", "ready in 1–3 years", or "long-term potential".

3. **Development Plans**

    o   Create tailored development programmes, including training, mentorship, and project assignments.
    o   Align with career aspirations and organisational needs.

4. **Succession Matrix**

    o   Use a visual chart to map roles, current incumbents, and identified successors, with readiness timelines.

5. **Contingency Plans**

    o   Include strategies for unexpected vacancies to ensure uninterrupted leadership.

Real-World Example

A technology firm leveraged a succession planning template to address the unexpected resignation of its CEO. By identifying a ready-now successor and initiating targeted development for future leadership candidates, the company avoided operational disruptions and reassured stakeholders of its governance stability.

Best Practices for Implementation

- **Annual Reviews**

  Regularly evaluate key roles, assess gaps, and update the succession plan to reflect organisational changes and emerging leaders.

- **Strategic Alignment**

  Ensure the succession plan supports the company's long-term goals, including diversity, innovation, and global expansion.

- **Engagement and Transparency**

  Communicate the plan to the board and key stakeholders while maintaining confidentiality regarding potential successors.

- **Leverage Technology**

  Use HR analytics tools to identify trends, track candidate progress, and optimise development initiatives.

- **Monitor and Measure**

  Periodically assess the effectiveness of the succession plan by tracking leadership transitions and candidate readiness.

7. ESG Reporting Framework: Driving Transparency and Accountability

Purpose

An ESG Reporting Framework facilitates transparent and consistent reporting on Environmental, Social, and Governance (ESG) metrics, enabling stakeholders to assess the company's sustainability efforts and governance practices.

Key Components

1. **Environmental Metrics**

   - Carbon Emissions: Track and report Scope 1, 2, and 3 emissions.
   - Resource Efficiency: Data on energy, water, and waste management.
   - Climate Initiatives: Progress on renewable energy adoption and net-zero goals.

2. **Social Metrics**

   - Diversity and Inclusion: Employee demographics, leadership diversity, and equity initiatives.
   - Community Impact: Philanthropic activities, volunteer programmes, and local engagement.
   - Workplace Safety: Health and safety metrics, including incident rates.

3. **Governance Metrics**

   - Board Composition: Details on independence, diversity, and expertise.
   - Ethics and Compliance: Anti-corruption measures and whistleblower policies.

- Executive Compensation: Links between pay and ESG performance.

4. **Alignment with Global Standards**

   - **Frameworks:** Adhere to recognised standards such as the Global Reporting Initiative (GRI), Sustainability Accounting Standards Board (SASB), and Task Force on Climate-related Financial Disclosures (TCFD).
   - **Comparability:** Use benchmarks to facilitate peer comparison.

Legal and Regulatory Considerations

- For publicly traded companies, ensure compliance with:

   - **Disclosure Regulations:** Examples include SEC rules in the U.S., EU Taxonomy, or UAE's ESR (Economic Substance Regulations).
   - **Investor Expectations:** Align with ESG priorities highlighted by institutional investors.

Best Practices for Implementation

- **Data Collection and Verification**

   - Use robust data systems to track ESG metrics.
   - Engage third-party assurance providers for credibility and accuracy.

- **Effective Communication**

   - Present data visually using graphs, dashboards, and heatmaps.
   - Include qualitative narratives to contextualise quantitative results.

- **Stakeholder Engagement**

  - Actively engage investors, customers, and employees in shaping ESG priorities.
  - Respond to feedback through iterative improvements.

- **Regular Updates**

  - Publish ESG reports annually or biannually to maintain transparency and relevance.

8. Compensation Philosophy Statement: Aligning Pay with Performance and Strategy

Purpose

A Compensation Philosophy Statement defines the principles and guidelines for executive compensation, ensuring alignment with company performance, long-term strategic goals, and shareholder interests. It establishes a framework to attract, retain, and motivate top talent while fostering accountability and ethical behaviour.

Key Components

1. **Performance Metrics**

   - Financial Metrics: Revenue growth, EBITDA, or profit margins to tie compensation to the company's financial health.
   - Non-Financial Metrics: Sustainability goals, customer satisfaction, and innovation-driven metrics, reflecting long-term value creation.
   - ESG Targets: Integration of environmental, social, and governance (ESG) objectives, such as carbon emissions reductions, diversity, and board governance improvements.

2. **Pay Structure**

   - Fixed Compensation: Base salary reflecting the role's scope and market competitiveness.
   - Variable Compensation: Performance-based bonuses and stock options to incentivise achieving set targets, including annual bonuses, long-term incentives, and equity awards.
   - Clawback Provisions: Clauses to reclaim compensation if financial statements are misstated or unethical conduct is identified.

3. **Equity Incentives**

    o   Stock Options/Restricted Stock Units (RSUs): Tied to long-term company performance and shareholder value, encouraging retention and alignment with long-term goals.

4. **Benchmarking**

    o   Industry Comparison: Compensation should be competitive with peers in the industry to attract and retain talent.
    o   Geographic Considerations: Compensation adjustments based on local market conditions and the cost of living for multinational companies.

Real-World Example

A renewable energy company implemented a compensation philosophy that ties executive bonuses to emission reduction targets and sustainability milestones, linking leadership incentives to the company's ESG priorities.

Best Practices for Implementation

- **Transparency in Reporting**

    o   Regularly disclose compensation policies, performance metrics, and executive pay packages in annual reports and proxy statements to ensure shareholder trust.

- **Annual Reviews**

    o   Regularly review the compensation strategy to adapt to changes in the business environment, market conditions, and corporate goals.

- **Shareholder Engagement**

    o   Actively engage with shareholders and proxy advisory firms to gain feedback on compensation structures.

- **Performance Periods**

  - Establish clear performance periods, typically ranging from 1 to 3 years for short-term incentives and 3 to 5 years for long-term performance-based equity awards.

9. Board Evaluation Questionnaire: Ensuring Effective Governance and Continuous Improvement

Purpose

The Board Evaluation Questionnaire is designed to assess the performance of the board as a whole and individual director. Its purpose is to identify areas of strength, uncover potential weaknesses, and provide actionable insights to enhance governance practices. Regular evaluations ensure efficient operations and foster continuous improvement.

Key Components

1. **Assessment of Board Effectiveness**

   - **Strategic Focus**: Evaluates how well the board oversees the company's strategic direction, including alignment with long-term goals.
   - **Decision-Making**: Assesses the timeliness and quality of the board's decision-making processes.
   - **Leadership**: Reviews the performance of the Chairperson and key leaders in guiding the board and the company.
   - **Board Composition**: Evaluates the board's mix of skills, diversity, and independence to meet company needs.

2. **Evaluation of Individual Directors**

   - **Engagement**: Assesses director participation, preparation, and contributions to discussions.
   - **Expertise and Contributions**: Measures effectiveness in guiding decision-making using specialised expertise.
   - **Relationship with Management**: Reviews the director's balance of independence and insightful support.

3. **Governance Practices**

   - **Board Dynamics**: Evaluates collaboration, discussion quality, and conflict resolution among board members.

- o **Committees**: Assesses committee effectiveness in fulfilling responsibilities and making impactful recommendations.

Best Practices

- **Anonymous Responses**: Ensure candid feedback by maintaining anonymity.
- **External Facilitators**: Use external experts for impartial evaluations.
- **Focus on Continuous Improvement**: Utilise results constructively for improvement.
- **Actionable Outcomes**: Develop and monitor action plans based on feedback.
- **Regular Frequency**: Conduct evaluations annually.

10. Executive Performance Review Template: Ensuring Accountability and Alignment with Company Goals

Purpose

This template assesses senior executives' performance to ensure alignment with organisational strategic objectives and key performance indicators (KPIs). It fosters accountability, professional growth, and leadership improvement.

Key Components

1. **Self-Assessment**

   - **Personal Reflection**: Executives evaluate their strengths, improvement areas, and progress.
   - **Goal Review**: Reflect on achievements and challenges against KPIs.
   - **Development Needs**: Identify required resources or training.

2. **Peer Feedback**

   - **360-Degree Feedback**: Gather input from senior management and direct reports.
   - **Interpersonal Skills**: Evaluate communication and conflict management abilities.
   - **Team Effectiveness**: Assess collaboration within leadership and the broader organisation.

3. **Board Evaluation**

   - **Alignment with Strategic Objectives**: Assess achievements in driving growth and shareholder value.
   - **Decision-Making and Leadership**: Evaluate ethical judgement, crisis management, and stewardship.
   - **Impact on Culture**: Review contributions to corporate values and ethics.

Best Practices

- Use structured and objective criteria.
- Conduct regular reviews with development plans.
- Incorporate 360-degree feedback.
- Link outcomes to compensation and career growth.

11. Independent Director's Charter

Purpose

Outlines the roles, responsibilities, and expectations of independent directors, emphasising impartial oversight, governance integrity, and conflict-free management.

Key Components

1. **Roles and Responsibilities**

   - **Risk Oversight**: Monitor strategic, operational, and financial risks.
   - **Stakeholder Interests**: Advocate for shareholder rights and alignment with long-term interests.
   - **Governance Oversight**: Assess board effectiveness, compliance, and internal controls.
   - **Financial Oversight**: Ensure financial transparency and audit integrity.

2. **Criteria for Independence**

   - **No Financial Ties**: Avoid significant income dependency or relationships with the company.
   - **No Personal Interests**: Exclude close familial or prior management roles.
   - **No Management Involvement**: Maintain distance from daily operations.

Best Practices

- Conduct periodic independence assessments.
- Provide training on governance and regulatory updates.
- Set term limits to ensure fresh perspectives.

12. Board Committee Charters

Purpose

Defines the purpose, authority, and responsibilities of board committees to ensure accountability and operational clarity.

Key Components

1. **Committee Purpose and Objectives**

    - Define the primary mandate of each committee.
    - Align objectives with regulatory requirements and organisational goals.

2. **Committee Membership**

    - Specify required skills and independence criteria.
    - Designate a chairperson for leadership and reporting.

3. **Authority and Decision-Making Power**

    - Outline the scope of authority, including resource access and decision-making capacity.

Best Practices

- Review charters annually to ensure relevance.
- Align committee roles with organisational strategy.
- Maintain independence and objectivity in critical committees.

13. Shareholder Rights Statement

Purpose

The Shareholder Rights Statement outlines the fundamental rights of shareholders in relation to their ownership of a company. This statement ensures transparency and equitable treatment for all shareholders, fostering trust and engagement. It is a key component in protecting shareholder interests and supporting good governance practices, helping the company maintain clear and open lines of communication with its shareholders.

Key Components

1. **Voting Rights**

   Shareholders typically have the right to vote on major corporate matters, including the election of directors, mergers, acquisitions, and significant corporate decisions. The voting mechanism can vary, with one-share, one-vote being the most common structure, although some companies may issue multiple classes of stock with different voting powers.

   Proxy Voting: In many jurisdictions, shareholders can vote through a proxy, allowing them to delegate their voting rights to another person or entity when unable to attend meetings. Clear provisions should be made for the submission of proxy votes.

2. **Dividend Entitlements**

   Shareholders have the right to receive dividends as determined by the company's board. The Shareholder Rights Statement should outline the criteria for dividend payments, how they are decided (e.g., based on company performance, retained earnings), and the expected frequency (e.g., quarterly, annually).

3. Access to Company Information

Shareholders are entitled to access information necessary for making informed decisions. This includes the annual financial statements, shareholder meeting minutes, and reports on the company's governance and strategy.

The statement should detail the processes by which shareholders can request access to information, the timeline for receiving it, and any confidentiality or disclosure limitations.

4. Shareholder Meetings

The statement should outline the rights of shareholders to attend, speak at, and vote during annual general meetings (AGMs) and extraordinary general meetings (EGMs). It should define the process for calling meetings, the minimum notice periods, and any thresholds for convening meetings (e.g. percentage of voting shares required).

In many companies, shareholder meetings are the primary venue for discussing important matters such as the election of directors, approval of financial reports, and approval of dividends. The Shareholder Rights Statement should ensure that meetings are held in a fair, timely, and transparent manner.

5. Shareholder Proposals

Shareholders may have the right to propose new business at shareholder meetings. The Shareholder Rights Statement should clearly define the process for submitting proposals, including required submission deadlines, shareholder eligibility criteria, and any required supporting documents.

6. Pre-Emptive Rights

Shareholders may have pre-emptive rights to purchase additional shares before they are offered to the public in the event of a new share issuance. This ensures that shareholders can maintain their proportional ownership in the company.

7. **Protection from Dilution**

The statement should outline any rights shareholders have in protecting their stake from dilution through new equity offerings, mergers, or acquisitions. For example, it may provide details on how shareholders are notified and how they can act to protect their interests.

8. **Legal Considerations**

Jurisdictional Compliance: The Shareholder Rights Statement must comply with the jurisdictional regulations where the company is incorporated. For example, under UAE Commercial Companies Law, shareholder rights must align with the provisions for corporate governance, minority shareholder protections, and financial disclosures. Similar regulations exist in other jurisdictions, such as the Companies Act in the UK or the Securities Exchange Act in the U.S., which set out rights regarding voting, dividends, and disclosure.

Fairness: It is critical that the Shareholder Rights Statement ensures that all shareholders, regardless of the size of their holdings, are treated fairly. The statement must also protect the rights of minority shareholders, particularly in scenarios involving mergers, acquisitions, or changes in company structure.

Best Practices

- **Regular Updates:** Regularly review and update the Shareholder Rights Statement to reflect changes in governance practices, legal requirements, and shareholder expectations. It should be updated in response to significant events such as mergers, IPOs, or changes in the company's capital structure.

- **Transparency and Communication**: Ensure that the Shareholder Rights Statement is clearly communicated to shareholders through multiple channels, including the company's website, shareholder communications, and during shareholder meetings. Transparency builds trust and allows shareholders to fully understand their rights. Regularly remind shareholders of their rights through email newsletters, quarterly updates, or dedicated sections on the company's website.

- **Easy Access to Information**: Ensure that all shareholders have easy access to key corporate documents, such as financial reports, governance policies, and meeting agendas. This can include making documents available in an online portal or sending copies upon request.

- **Clear Proxy Voting Process**: Clearly define the proxy voting process, including deadlines for submitting proxies, how proxies are handled, and how shareholders can assign their votes. Proxy forms should be easy to complete and accessible to all shareholders.

- **Annual Review**: Conduct an annual review of the Shareholder Rights Statement, ensuring that it remains aligned with both best practices in corporate governance and the company's business objectives. This review should also consider shareholder feedback and any changes in applicable law or industry standards.

14. Corporate Governance Checklist

Purpose

The Corporate Governance Checklist serves as a tool for organisations to assess their compliance with governance standards and identify areas for improvement. It ensures that a company adheres to legal, regulatory, and ethical practices, fostering transparency, accountability, and trust among stakeholders. Regular use of this checklist helps boards stay aligned with best practices and ensures the organisation's governance framework remains robust and effective.

Key Components

1. **Board Composition**

   - **Board Size and Diversity:** Ensure the board has an appropriate size to support decision-making while maintaining diversity in skills, experience, and backgrounds.
   - **Independent Directors:** Verify that the board includes a sufficient number of independent directors to provide objective oversight, ensuring their independence from management and major shareholders.
   - **Board Committees:** Review the composition and effectiveness of key board committees, including audit, compensation, and nominating/governance committees. Ensure these committees are staffed with members who possess relevant expertise.
   - **Director Qualifications and Experience:** Evaluate whether board members possess the necessary skills and experience to make informed decisions and guide the company's strategy effectively.

2. **Risk Management**

   - **Risk Identification:** Ensure that a formal process is in place to identify strategic, operational, financial, and compliance risks.

- ○ **Risk Oversight:** Evaluate how risks are monitored by the board and committees, including the use of risk dashboards and regular risk reports.
- ○ **Crisis Management:** Assess whether the organisation has crisis management plans in place and whether the board reviews these plans regularly.
- ○ **Compliance with Regulatory Standards:** Ensure the organisation complies with all local and international regulations related to governance, finance, and environmental practices.

3. **Shareholder Engagement**

- ○ **Shareholder Rights:** Confirm that the company has mechanisms to ensure shareholders' rights are protected, including voting rights, access to information, and involvement in key decisions.
- ○ **Shareholder Communication:** Assess the quality and transparency of communication with shareholders, including the frequency and format of shareholder meetings and disclosures.
- ○ **Shareholder Activism:** Evaluate the company's readiness to address concerns from activist shareholders or proxy advisory firms.

4. **Legal and Regulatory Requirements**

- ○ **Compliance with Corporate Laws:** Verify that the company complies with relevant corporate governance laws and regulations, such as the UAE Commercial Companies Law or the U.S. Sarbanes-Oxley Act.
- ○ **Regulatory Filings:** Ensure the company submits necessary reports to regulatory authorities on time, including financial statements, shareholder disclosures, and board activities.

- ○ **Public Disclosure:** Ensure the company meets transparency requirements in its financial and non-financial reporting, including disclosures on executive compensation, environmental impact, and corporate social responsibility initiatives.

Real-World Example

A financial services company uses the checklist to prepare for its annual governance audit. The audit team assesses whether the company complies with regulatory standards, evaluates the effectiveness of risk management frameworks, and reviews shareholder engagement practices. Based on the checklist results, the company identifies areas for improvement, such as enhancing board diversity and improving crisis management preparedness, and implements changes accordingly.

Best Practices

- **Tailor the Checklist to Specific Regulatory Frameworks:** Adapt the checklist to reflect the governance and regulatory requirements specific to the industry and jurisdiction in which the company operates. For example, a financial institution will have different governance requirements compared to a technology startup.
- **Use the Checklist as a Living Document:** The checklist should not be a one-time tool but a living document that is regularly updated to reflect changes in regulations, corporate practices, and company strategies. This ensures continuous improvement in governance and keeps the company compliant with evolving standards.
- **Regularly Review and Update:** Governance practices and regulatory requirements change over time, so it's essential to regularly review and update the checklist to ensure it remains relevant and effective. This can be done on an annual basis or

whenever significant changes occur within the organisation or its operating environment.

- **Incorporate Feedback from Stakeholders**: Regularly seek feedback from key stakeholders, including board members, management, shareholders, and external auditors, to ensure the checklist reflects their concerns and expectations. This fosters a culture of accountability and transparency across the organisation.

- **Track Progress and Document Findings**: Use the checklist not only for assessing compliance but also for tracking progress on governance improvements. Document findings from each assessment and ensure that they are communicated effectively to relevant stakeholders, including the board, management, and key decision-makers. This documentation should highlight areas of strength, identify gaps, and outline actionable recommendations, serving as a roadmap for continuous improvement in governance practices. By maintaining a clear record of progress, organisations can ensure accountability, measure the impact of changes over time, and foster a culture of transparency and commitment to excellence.

15. Proxy Statement

Purpose

A Proxy Statement is a critical document that provides shareholders with comprehensive information about important matters to be voted on during a shareholder meeting. It ensures transparency by disclosing significant corporate decisions, such as director elections, executive compensation, and proposed corporate actions. By doing so, it empowers shareholders to make informed decisions about their involvement and voting in the company's governance.

Key Components

1. **Director Nominations**

   - **Nominee Information**: Provides detailed profiles of nominated directors, including their background, experience, and qualifications.
   - **Board Composition**: Explains the rationale behind the proposed nominations, such as ensuring a diverse skill set or filling gaps in expertise.
   - **Independence**: Discloses whether nominated directors meet independence requirements, if applicable, and their role in overseeing management.

2. **Executive Compensation**

   - **Compensation Structure**: Describes the compensation philosophy, including salary, bonuses, stock options, and other benefits.
   - **Performance Metrics**: Links executive compensation to key performance indicators (KPIs) such as revenue growth, profit margins, and strategic achievements (e.g., mergers, acquisitions).
   - **Disclosure of Changes**: Informs shareholders of any significant changes to executive compensation, such as

increases or new bonuses linked to company performance or strategic objectives.

3. **Corporate Actions**

    o   **Mergers and Acquisitions**: Provides details of any proposed mergers, acquisitions, or divestitures, including the strategic rationale behind the actions.

    o   **Stock Issuances or Buybacks**: Informs shareholders about any plans for issuing additional shares or repurchasing company stock.

    o   **Corporate Restructuring**: Outlines major changes to the company's structure, including reorganisations, business unit sales, or spin-offs.

4. **Voting Procedures**

    o   **Instructions for Voting**: Explains how shareholders can vote on the matters included in the proxy statement, including methods such as voting by proxy, online, or by mail.

    o   **Meeting Date and Location**: Provides details about the shareholder meeting, including time, date, and venue (or virtual meeting instructions).

    o   **Quorum and Voting Thresholds**: Specifies the minimum number of shares required for quorum and the voting thresholds needed for resolutions to pass.

Real-World Example

A retail company uses its proxy statement to disclose a CEO compensation increase tied to specific performance goals, such as store expansion. The statement provides shareholders with clear metrics, including target store openings and revenue growth expectations, which will trigger the compensation increase. This transparency helps shareholders understand the strategic alignment between executive incentives and company growth.

Best Practices

- **Ensure Compliance with Disclosure Requirements**

  Adhere to local and international regulations governing shareholder communications, such as those from the Securities and Exchange Commission (SEC) in the U.S. or other regulatory bodies in different jurisdictions. This ensures that the proxy statement meets legal standards and is fully compliant.

- **Clear and Transparent Language**

  Use clear, non-technical language to explain complex matters. Avoid jargon that could confuse shareholders. Ensure that executive compensation and other sensitive topics are explained in a straightforward and transparent manner to build trust with shareholders.

- **Make the Document Visually Engaging**

  Structure the proxy statement with visually engaging elements such as tables, graphs, and charts to present financial information and compensation breakdowns. This enhances readability and allows shareholders to digest important information quickly.

- **Timely Distribution**

  Distribute the proxy statement well in advance of the shareholder meeting—typically at least 30 days before the meeting. This allows shareholders ample time to review the document, consult with advisers, and vote accordingly.

- **Highlight Key Issues**

  In addition to presenting all relevant information, highlight key issues that shareholders need to focus on, such as proposed executive compensation increases, mergers, or acquisitions. This can be done using sidebars, callout boxes, or summary sections.

- **Incorporate Digital Features**

  Consider offering a digital version of the proxy statement that shareholders can easily access online. Incorporate interactive features such as online voting options and detailed explanatory links to make it easier for shareholders to engage.

- **Engage Shareholders with Summary Sections**

  Include an executive summary at the beginning of the document to quickly inform shareholders of the most important items. This will help them focus on the key topics without needing to read through the entire document.

16. Board Member Orientation Manual

Purpose:

The Board Member Orientation Manual serves as a comprehensive guide for introducing new directors to the company and their key responsibilities. This document is designed to ensure that new board members understand the organisation's mission, strategic goals, financial position, and governance practices. By equipping new directors with essential knowledge, the manual helps them integrate effectively into the board and contribute to the company's long-term success.

Key Components:

1. **Overview of the Company's Mission, Strategy, and Financials**

   - **Mission Statement:** An introduction to the company's purpose, core values, and long-term vision.
   - **Strategic Goals:** A detailed explanation of the company's strategic initiatives, market positioning, and growth plans.
   - **Financial Overview:** Key financial metrics, including recent performance, financial health, and any significant financial challenges or opportunities.
   - **Business Model:** A brief description of the company's revenue streams, key products or services, and target markets.

2. **Board Policies, Procedures, and Governance Framework**

   - **Board Responsibilities:** An outline of the board's roles and duties, including fiduciary responsibilities, decision-making authority, and involvement in key corporate actions.
   - **Governance Structure:** A description of the company's governance framework, including the separation of powers between the board and management.

- o **Board Committees:** Information on various board committees (e.g., Audit, Compensation, Governance) and their respective responsibilities.
- o **Meeting Procedures:** A guide to how board meetings are structured, including agenda setting, voting processes, and meeting protocols.
- o **Ethical Guidelines and Compliance:** An overview of the company's code of conduct, compliance expectations, and conflict of interest policies.

3. **Company Culture and Expectations**

- o **Board Dynamics:** A brief on board culture, communication expectations, and the importance of collegiality and open discussion.
- o **Engagement with Stakeholders:** Guidance on how board members should engage with shareholders, employees, regulators, and other key stakeholders.
- o **Performance Expectations:** Clear expectations regarding board member involvement, meeting attendance, preparation, and contribution to strategic discussions.

4. **Key Industry Regulations**

- o **Legal and Regulatory Environment:** A primer on the relevant industry regulations, corporate governance codes, and compliance requirements that impact the board's operations.
- o **Sector-Specific Issues:** An overview of key trends, challenges, and opportunities within the company's specific industry.

Hypothetical Scenario:

A new director joins the board of a healthcare organisation. They use the orientation manual to familiarise themselves with the company's mission of providing quality healthcare services while maintaining profitability. The manual provides insights into the company's expansion plans into new markets, a recent shift in regulatory compliance requirements in healthcare, and the board's specific role in overseeing such strategic decisions. The new director also learns about key industry regulations, such as patient privacy laws and healthcare accreditation standards, helping them understand their responsibilities.

Best Practices:

- **Include a Glossary of Key Terms and Acronyms**

  A glossary is essential to help new directors familiarise themselves with industry jargon, corporate governance terminology, and abbreviations commonly used in the company's operations. This aids in ensuring effective communication during board discussions.

- **Provide Digital Access for Ease of Reference**

  Offering a digital version of the orientation manual ensures that board members have easy access to this essential document. A digital format allows for real-time updates, interactive content, and hyperlinks to other relevant documents (e.g., the company's financial reports, board meeting minutes). This ensures that directors can reference it anytime they need to clarify a point or refresh their memory.

- **Periodic Updates and Continuous Education**

  The orientation manual should be updated regularly to reflect changes in governance practices, company strategy, and legal requirements. Additionally, providing ongoing education through board training sessions can further equip new directors with deeper insights into their roles.

- **Encourage Engagement and Interaction**

  New directors should be encouraged to actively engage with existing board members and management, attend site visits, and participate in informal briefings to enhance their understanding of the company and its operations. A mentorship programme can also be beneficial for guiding new members through their initial period.

17. Director's Information Form

Purpose:

The Director's Information Form is designed to collect biographical, professional, and financial details about board members to ensure transparency and compliance with governance standards. This form helps the company assess potential conflicts of interest, evaluate a director's qualifications, and maintain an accurate record of board members' affiliations and financial interests. It is an essential tool for safeguarding the integrity of the board and ensuring alignment with legal and regulatory requirements.

Key Components:

1. **Educational Qualifications and Experience**

     o **Academic Background:** A section to capture the director's educational qualifications, including degrees, certifications, and relevant professional training.

     o **Professional Experience:** Information about the director's career history, including past and present positions held, areas of expertise, and leadership roles within other organisations.

2. **Disclosure of Conflicts of Interest**

     o **Conflicts of Interest:** A detailed disclosure of any financial or personal interests that might create conflicts of interest with the director's role on the board. This includes investments in competitors, suppliers, or any other entities that may affect the director's impartiality.

     o **Related Party Transactions:** Information on any transactions involving the director, their family, or related entities that might be relevant to the company's operations.

3. **Directorships in Other Companies**

    ○   **Other Board Positions:** A section where the director lists any current or past directorships in other companies, including both public and private companies. This is important to ensure there is no overlap of interests or potential conflicts due to other commitments.

    ○   **Time Commitment:** Directors are also asked to estimate the time commitment required for each of their other board roles to ensure they can dedicate sufficient time to their responsibilities.

4. **Financial Interests and Holdings**

    ○   **Equity Interests:** Any equity or financial interests in the company, including stock ownership, options, or other forms of financial investment.

    ○   **Compensation:** Details of compensation, such as fees or other remuneration from the company, to ensure transparency in the director's financial relationship with the company.

Real-World Example:

In a recent case, a director was appointed to the board of a publicly traded company. During the disclosure process via the Director's Information Form, it was revealed that the director had an undisclosed financial interest in a direct competitor. This raised potential conflicts of interest and prompted the company to reconsider the director's appointment, ensuring that the integrity of board decisions was not compromised.

Best Practices:

- **Keep Forms Confidential but Accessible for Compliance Reviews**

  The information disclosed in the Director's Information Form must be treated with the highest level of confidentiality. However, it should also be readily accessible for compliance reviews, especially during regulatory audits or when evaluating potential conflicts of interest. Secure storage systems, such as encrypted files, are essential to protect sensitive information.

- **Use Standardised Templates for Consistency**

  To maintain consistency and ease of review, companies should use standardised templates for the Director's Information Form. This ensures that all necessary information is captured in a uniform format, making it easier to compare disclosures across multiple board members and streamline the compliance process.

- **Annual Updates**

  Directors should be required to update their information on an annual basis or whenever there are significant changes in their professional or financial circumstances. This helps ensure that the board's records remain current and accurate.

- **Regular Review and Monitoring**

  The company's corporate governance team should regularly review the disclosures to identify potential conflicts of interest or any discrepancies in the information provided. Proactive monitoring helps maintain transparency and ensures compliance with legal and ethical standards.

- **Incorporate into Director Onboarding**

  The Director's Information Form should be a key component of the onboarding process for new directors. Completing the form early in their appointment ensures that all required information is gathered before they begin their official duties on the board.

18. Board Meeting Etiquette Guidelines

Purpose:

The Board Meeting Etiquette Guidelines establish a framework for maintaining respectful, effective, and productive board meetings. These guidelines promote professionalism and a collaborative atmosphere, ensuring that meetings run smoothly, decisions are made efficiently, and conflicts are handled constructively. Adhering to these etiquette principles enhances board dynamics, fostering trust and ensuring alignment with the organisation's governance values.

Key Components:

1. **Punctuality**

   Board members are expected to arrive on time and be prepared for all meetings. Punctuality demonstrates respect for others' time and ensures that discussions begin promptly, allowing for full participation in all agenda items.

2. **Preparation**

   Directors should come to meetings having reviewed all relevant materials, including the meeting agenda, financial reports, and any supporting documents. Preparedness enhances the quality of discussions and ensures that decision-making is informed and efficient.

3. **Active Listening and Respectful Communication**

   Directors should engage in active listening, giving each speaker the opportunity to express their views without interruption. When speaking, directors should do so clearly and respectfully, addressing issues directly rather than making personal comments.

4. **Focus on the Agenda**

   Discussions should remain focused on the agenda and the specific issues at hand. Directors should avoid straying into unrelated topics, as this can dilute the effectiveness of the meeting and waste valuable time.

5. **Constructive Debate**

   Board meetings should be a forum for constructive debate, where differing opinions are encouraged and addressed respectfully. Disagreements should be resolved professionally, with a focus on finding common ground and making decisions in the best interest of the company.

Real-World Example:

In a recent board meeting, directors were able to resolve a major disagreement over a proposed strategic initiative through respectful and constructive debate. While the differing opinions were strongly expressed, each director listened carefully, asked clarifying questions, and worked collaboratively to arrive at a consensus. This approach not only resulted in a better decision but also strengthened the board's cohesion.

Best Practices:

- **Pre-Meeting Briefing**

  Providing directors with a pre-meeting briefing helps ensure they come prepared. This may include a call or email to review key discussion points and clarify any ambiguities in the meeting agenda.

- **Use of Technology**

  With the increasing reliance on virtual meetings, directors should familiarise themselves with the relevant technology to ensure that virtual board meetings are as effective as in-person ones. This includes understanding the features of video conferencing tools, muting when not speaking, and ensuring a stable internet connection.

- **Time Management**

To maintain focus and efficiency, the meeting chair should adhere to time limits for each agenda item. This helps prevent any one topic from dominating the discussion and ensures that all key issues are addressed.

- **Conflict Resolution Mechanisms**

In the event of a disagreement or conflict, the chair should intervene to maintain decorum and guide the discussion toward a resolution. Implementing conflict resolution strategies ensures that the board remains unified and focused on its strategic goals.

Notes